The Courage to Ride

A legendary 17,000 mile ride from Argentina to Canada

by

Ana Beker

The Long Riders' Guild Press

www.thelongridersguild.com

ISBN: 1-59048-041-4

To the Reader:

The editors and publishers of The Long Riders' Guild Press faced significant technical and financial difficulties in bringing this and the other titles in the Equestrian Travel Classics collection to the light of day.

Though the authors represented in this international series envisioned their stories being shared for generations to come, all too often that was not the case. Sadly, many of the books now being published by The Long Riders' Guild Press were discovered gracing the bookshelves of rare book dealers, adorned with princely prices that placed them out of financial reach of the common reader. The remainder were found lying neglected on the scrap heap of history, their once-proud stories forgotten, their once-glorious covers stained by the toil of time and a host of indifferent previous owners.

However The Long Riders' Guild Press passionately believes that this book, and its literary sisters, remain of global interest and importance. We stand committed, therefore, to bringing our readers the best copy of these classics at the most affordable price. The copy which you now hold may have small blemishes originating from the master text.

We apologize in advance for any defects of this nature.

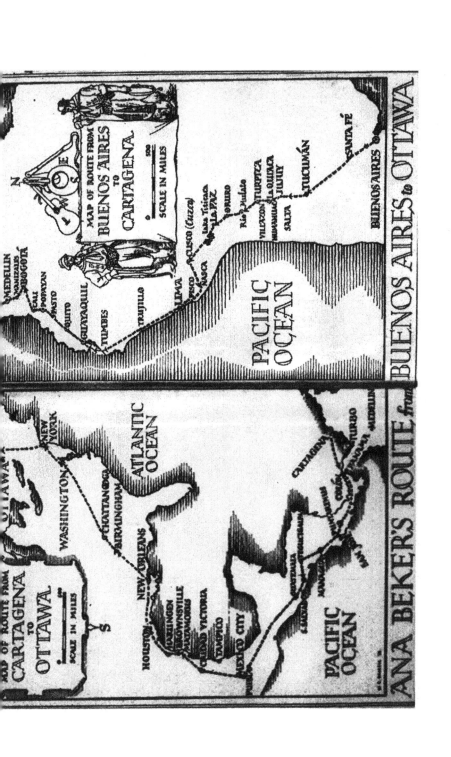

ANA BEKER'S ROUTE from BUENOS AIRES to OTTAWA

Full-dress entry at Victoria, Mexico.

I have to thank the author Clemente Cimorra for his most valuable aid in preparing this true narrative of my journey for publication.

ANA BEKER.

Translated from the Spanish
by
JAMES CLEUGH

CONTENTS

LIST OF ILLUSTRATIONS

CHAPTER I

DREAMS OF A PLANTER'S DAUGHTER

THE two things that impressed me most as a little girl were the solitude of the open country, the great, treeless, grassy plains of the *pampas*, and the sight of that friendly and beautiful animal, the horse, free to range at will over the open pastures.

It is difficult to describe the unbroken plains of Argentina to those who dwell in towns or in different country. I have heard of the passion of sailors for the sea; the *pampa* resembles a green sea and, like the sea, it is never the same; for us who were brought up on it, the details of its appearance and the secrets it hides change continually.

My parents were country-bred Lithuanians, who had bought a small estate in Argentina. I was born on an estate near Loberia, some 250 miles south of Buenos Aires. I accompanied my parents in their search for better land and was eventually brought up at Algaroba in the Villarino district.

When I was four years old I was already hugging the legs of the foals that were born and grew up on the estate; I have always loved horses and especially the spirited thoroughbred. While still scarcely more than a child I used to get up in the middle of the night to take the horses to drink. My father several times forbade me to do it and I had to put up with some severe lectures for the trouble I took on their behalf but I simply couldn't keep away from them. I loved to ride bare-backed, in contact with their cool, satiny hides under the glittering starlight to the nocturnal music of toads and crickets. I enjoyed, too, the feeling that the horses were being properly looked after as they deserved. I could never bring myself to forget them at night; I shouldn't have been able to sleep if I had thought they were liable to undergo any discomfort.

[Of all our horses the one I liked best, when I was a child, was a pony with a white streak on the forehead; he was far more friendly and companionable than any boy of my own age would have been. I kept him so well groomed that his hide shone like silk; when I rode him, he enjoyed the gallop as much as I did.

Another thing that worried me a lot was the invariable catchphrase I heard whenever I referred to anything not in the day's work or to any problem that was bothering me. 'That's a *man's* business,' they always used to say. Even when I wanted to ride in a gymkhana I had to give up the idea because 'a woman's best employed when she's getting the *mate* (South American tea) ready'. I used to declare even then that a South American woman would be perfectly capable of taking on jobs that would make some of the toughest males recoil. As time went on I became obsessed with the idea of proving my words.

When I reached marriageable age I quarrelled with several would-be suitors on account of their views on the weakness and helplessness of women, which I resented and could not let pass unchallenged. Even with the man I most liked there were incessant disputes and arguments on this perennial subject. Whenever he saw me galloping along with the stockmen and beating them in the race after a herd of horses or cattle, he reproved me for being so crazy as to try to rival men at a job I was not capable of doing.

On one occasion I was invited with others from the estate to an ostrich hunt. Everyone assumed without question that I was simply going, like the other girls and the married women, to help with the roasting of the game and in other similar tasks; but no sooner had the horsemen begun to close in on the chosen area and prepare their weapons, the leathern thongs with leaden balls attached to them, and the first birds got up from the tall grass than I started riding with the men and actually set off in pursuit of an ostrich that was racing along in a panic, using wings as well as feet. Everyone thought I had stayed behind with the spare mounts brought by the party and, though they appreciated the bold display of horsemanship, they resented my interference in 'a man's business'.

Years passed; my eyes were perpetually fixed on the horizon of the pampas and that contemptuous attitude to women remained a perpetual thorn in my flesh. At last I began to plan my first adventure in the outside world. At that time the chief place of pilgrimage, in that part of the country, was the town of Lujan, which possessed a beautiful church dedicated to the Virgin. There were stories of heroic vows, the details of which may have been true or invented, which had been duly fulfilled by people who had ridden continuously for weeks on end. I decided to set myself the first test of my vocation as a horsewoman by riding to Lujan and was determined to succeed in getting there. The journey seemed little more than child's play to me at that time; my familiarity with horses had accustomed me to regard any adventure undertaken in the company of a good horse as nothing to worry about.

When I told my friends that I meant to ride the distance of nearly 900 miles between La Pampa and Lujan alone on my horse Clavel ('Carnation'), they looked at me as though I had just been let out of a lunatic asylum. Then they invariably protested. "Why? Whatever for?" In reply I informed them that I wished to prove, in however modest a fashion, that a woman could carry out any project she had once determined upon, and also that a first-rate plantation horse would be perfectly fresh after any number of days' riding.

I reached Lujan in nineteen days, without any particular trouble; I felt intensely proud of my success and flung my arms round the neck of the sorrel.

Many people congratulated me, though they did not fail to advise me not to make any further attempts at having my name recorded in the "annals of chivalry". As for my own family, their verdict was that I must never do such a mad thing again for it would be tempting Providence. The upshot of it all was that the entire neighbourhood began to oppose my plans for further feats on horseback even more vigorously than before I went to Lujan.

Against this advice I immediately began to plan my second ride. It was to be a much more daring and elaborate one, very far indeed from being 'a woman's affair' and scarcely even that of a full-fledged male. My longing to travel, which also influenced the schemes I had in mind, suggested that I should begin by exploring the fourteen provinces of my own most beautiful country. I set myself to draw up an itinerary for the purpose. In my researches I soon found that I met with nothing but hostility or blank incomprehension—in the majority of cases, indeed, an icy incredulity and indifference. I was told practically the same thing everywhere, that what I intended to do could only be done by a man, and an exceptional man at that. Everywhere I went people shrugged their shoulders. Even in circles where one would naturally expect to find encouragement for such proposals—clubs and societies, for instance, concerned with horses—I was refused assistance which would enable me to carry out my plans.

But though all other doors were closed against me, President Ortiz, who was then head of the Government, told me that if I were so keen on proving that a woman could perform the tasks of a man he would provide me with the indispensable official aid for making the attempt.

I was thus able to pick two horses of the pure South American breed, a dappled grey called Zorzal ('Thrush") and a sorrel that answered to the name of Ranchero ('Rancher'). I set off with these two, full of high hopes and optimism, amid the laughter of many who saw me go and polite expressions of good wishes on the part of others. For ten months I rode through the rich and varied landscape of my country, ending my tour in 1942.

This journey through the provinces of Argentina prepared me most effectually for future schemes, such as that of exploring the entire continent. It was a great help, in my design of getting to know the world, to survey the diversity of climates and scenes offered by my own native land. They varied from the exuberance of the forests, with their waterfalls, and the heat that accounts for the prolific vegetation of the region in the north-east of the country, to the impressive monotony of La Pampa, where only the shadow of the sugar-cane interrupts mile after mile of level plain.

My horses and I passed the mighty aqueducts of Tucumán, the garden of the Republic, threading our way through paradisal valleys and also crossing the triple barriers of the Cordoba mountains, that picturesque group which gladdens the eye of the traveller, while its lakes and torrents refresh his spirit. It was hard going in many places, as among the knife-edge ridges and the bogs of Entre Rios, but we were rewarded at last for our pains by the great rolling plains, the ever fertile and resurgent pastures of the province of Buenos Aires.

When I set to work in earnest on the greatest of all my projects I found I was in for a colossal struggle; it lasted even longer than the whole of the journey itself, for success in the latter depended on myself alone, while in the former the outcome was determined by others. It was nobody's business to instruct me in what I had to do; I knew what I wanted to achieve and I knew how I was going to set about it. If only those who could have made even the slightest effort to render my 'expedition' practicable had shown an equal measure of understanding!

When I tried to explain that what I had in mind was quite possible I was met by retorts similar to that voiced by the Argentine Riders' Society—"Even a man could hardly do such a thing, to say nothing of yourself."

"But anyone," I protested, "can do it who is sufficiently determined and not afraid of any risk he may run."

I prolonged my efforts for a whole ten years. The stumbling-block was invariably the same old dogmatic statement that no woman, and certainly not a woman travelling alone, could possibly make the journey from Buenos Aires to Ottawa, from Argentina to Canada, simply with two horses. Even my own family said that I was out of my mind.

I said to one of those who laughed loudest at my plan, a man about thirty who fancied himself as a horseman—"Let's each mount, side by side, and then you follow me till one of us can't stand it any longer and suggests riding back.''

That valiant horseman, who was so amused by 'girlish fancies', declined to accept the challenge.

One day I went to hear a lecture by the Swiss-born Aimé Felix Tschiffely, who had been a schoolmaster in the Argentine town of Quilmes, and had performed the feat of riding from Buenos Aires to New York with his two horses Mancha ('Spot') and Gato ('Cat') who all became world-famous after their achievement of the journey. He gave a full account, accompanied by pictures, of his progress over 10,000 miles of marshes, rivers, mountains, fenland, forest and desert in the New World.

After the lecture I obtained an interview with 'Chifeli', as he was generally called, and told him that I was planning to travel with one saddle-horse and a pack-horse to the capital of Canada. He stared at me for a moment in amazement. Then his characteristic, indulgent smile appeared. He expressed the view that if I succeeded in my plan, which would be extremely difficult to carry out, the feat would surpass his own, its great superiority being due to the fact that it would have been accomplished by a woman. He added that his own journey had brought him an invitation from the Geographical Society of the United States to give a formal lecture of the kind only previously admitted in the cases of the explorers Amundsen and Admiral Byrd. He then gave me this advice:

"Well, at any rate, if you do decide to go, avoid Bolivia. It's practically impossible to cross all those marshes and stony deserts.''

All I answered was: "You went that way, didn't you? So there's no reason why I shouldn't.''

In the end I decided, since I had already waited so long, to play my last card. I determined to take a chance and start there and then, with or without assistance. I was only short of one essential, indispensable item: the horses. They would have to be very strong and hardy, fit for the terrific test they would be undergoing.

Finally two men, with typical *gaucho* generosity, did me

the honour of taking me seriously and coming to my rescue. Thanks to their kindness I found myself the possessor of two magnificent animals, both sorrels, one with a white streak on the forehead. Their names were Principe ('Prince') and Churrito ('Shaggy'). The latter, a lively seven year old, was given to me by Manuel Andrada, the famous 'Farmer Andrada' who had become a champion polo-player after riding as a *gaucho*. The other animal, which was the same age, came from the stable of another great South American horseman, Don Pedro Mack. The horse he presented me with was a fine animal but difficult to handle; great efforts were still being made to train it for the saddle. I immediately took a liking to both animals and began training them for my own purposes, stabling them at the Mounted Police headquarters in Buenos Aires, where they were honoured guests and well looked after by express permission of the Chief of Police at that time, General Bertollo.

For six months I took these two for gallops, working them hard to give them the necessary toughness, till the day came when I could consider them fit for the gruelling adventure before us.

I had not troubled much about publicity for my plans, but they were pretty well known in equestrian circles and in Buenos Aires generally. Journalists came to see me and told me that my courage and determination were almost incredible in a girl of my age. They pointed out to me, with a certain amount of irony, that my proposal could not be considered in the light of a holiday week-end's riding; they reminded me that even if one went by train or the normal means of road transport a journey to Canada would be pretty tiring. They added that the mere thought of the mode of travel I myself intended to employ made them shudder.

"On horseback," they told me, "and with another horse coming along behind with your luggage, every mile is going to seem like a thousand. If you cover the distance you have in mind—assuming that you have plenty of luck and find yourself physically capable of it—no one will ever be able to beat your record."

"Not unless they go from Tierra del Fuego to Alaska," I retorted. "And even that wouldn't be much more strenuous. I'm not going to attempt any such thing, myself. My idea is simply to link up the two capital cities of the continent which are furthest apart."

The same journalists informed me that all former exploits on horseback would be eclipsed by mine. I felt encouraged by their enthusiasm, so different from the pessimistic prophecies I was used to from others. Ever since then I have always kept a warm place in my heart for journalists. One of them declared that the horse is the best friend of man. Another went one better by adding: "And of woman, too, as we can see in this case, when a woman is going to show us men up as no better than a lot of kids."

CHAPTER II

THE FIRST MILE

O N the 1st of October, 1950, I decided that it was time to start. I set out on my first mile from the beautiful square in Buenos Aires in which the Congress building is situated. I was dressed in the *gaucho* fashion, with baggy trousers, riding-boots, a wide-brimmed hat and a brightly coloured scarf wound round the neck.

Representatives of the Press, photographers and enthusiastic members of the public gave me a rousing send-off. Marcelino Soule, an expert horseman and traveller, who afterwards took up motor-racing and lost his life on the track, came to wish me a good journey.

I expressed my most grateful thanks to all who had come to see me off and to all who had facilitated the initial stage of my undertaking. I mentioned particularly the Mounted Police of the capital, in whose quarters my horses had been so marvellously well cared for and who had given me so much encouragement.

Some of my family also came to say good-bye, though in the rather more literal sense of the word, as if taking leave of me for ever: their attitude appeared to be that of persons facing the imminent loss of a close relative.

It was only I myself who enjoyed the thrill of departure and the certainty that my dream was now at last to be realised. As I left behind me the boisterous clamour of the streets of the busy seaport I longed to breathe again the air of the wide open spaces.

A number of people on horseback rode with me as far as San Isidro in the suburbs. I felt that I should soon be alone with my two four-footed companions and for the future would have to rely on myself at every turn of the road.

But this excellent start was not destined to last very long. I had no sooner settled down to a steady progress along Road 9, leading out of the city, when my first mishap occurred in a somewhat alarming manner. My pack-horse had been tied to the girth of the one I was riding. In the bustle and confusion of my departure I had not noticed that this mistake had been made.

The pack-horse suddenly tugged at the girth with all its strength, startled my mount and the latter threw me. The impact of my fall was so violent and unexpected against the hard surface of the road that I lost consciousness and only came to in hospital at San Fernando. When I opened my eyes, the first question I asked was:

"Where are they?"

"Where are who, señorita?"

"Churrito and Principe, my horses."

I was told that they were perfectly all right. Of course someone added: "That wasn't a very good start, was it? Enough to discourage most people."

"Not at all," I retorted. "It was simply a warning. It makes me all the keener to get on."

One fine morning, with renewed enthusiasm, I rejoined my horses which neighed with delight at the sight of me and set off once more towards the open spaces and towns of Argentina, heading north. I was bound for an America of which I knew very little, and for whatever surprises that vast continent might have in store for me.

I had already, during this first stage of my ride through my native land, to take the precautions necessary for a life in the wilds. It is not easy to calculate how far one can get by nightfall and therefore difficult to choose a stopping-place. During the first long days of riding one's horses are liable to get over-exhausted if one asks more of them than they are used to doing.

My whole project depended on my horses not being deprived of their essential needs, and I foresaw that one of my greatest difficulties was going to be concerned with their maintenance. A human being can exist on almost anything, on fruit taken from a tree at the side of the road, on a little meat that may be offered by some local inhabitant, on a handful of green maize or half a tomato; human beings can carry on for several days without eating and for many hours without drinking. But such an animal as a horse needs large quantities of food of more or less the same kind and plenty of water. This problem had always been a great worry to me, ever since both first-hand enquiry and geographical research had convinced me that I should have to ride for countless miles through places where there would not be a blade of grass for the horses to eat.

The great distances involved in this first stage of my journey towards the north of Argentina, though the roads were good and the scenery of the rich countryside with its unending procession of fields of growing crops and pastures delighted the eye, made me realise that whole days in the saddle can be pretty tiring.

After reaching my first objective, the populous and busy town of Rosario, I began to cross the fertile plain of Santa Fe. The shimmering pampas was familiar to me and I enjoyed the prospect of the spacious and fruitful landscape, which as a child I had loved more than any other. People living in large cities can have no idea of the tranquillity of those great solitudes, which can only really be appreciated in travelling through them at leisure; nothing but thousands of acres covered for mile after mile by herds and flocks quietly grazing.

Parties of men at work on the plains would often call a jovial greeting to me as they saw me ride purposefully past, dressed like a true *gaucho*, and followed by the pack-horse, which indicated that I was on a long journey. Some of them would shout facetiously:

"Where's the farmer's daughter off to, then, in that rig-out as if she were never coming back?" or, "Better hurry, lady! We're not so well off for golden-haired *gaucho* girls in this part of the country!"

I would sometimes turn aside to visit farm-buildings, where I would be offered accommodation for the horses and a lodging for the night. I used to enjoy sitting round the stove with the cattlemen, talking away while the *bombilla*, the metal tube through which *mate* is drunk, passed from hand to hand and the agreeable odour of roast meat filled the room. When they asked me what I was doing on the road I tried to make them understand, by totting up the miles or comparing the distances with those they knew, how far I was going. One old rustic after a careful inspection of my horses observed:

"With a pair like that, if you feed them both equally well, stay in country like this and give them all the rest they need, you'll reach your destination all right. But I shouldn't care to buy them after you've got there."

I was given a lot of advice both seriously and as a joke. "Did you ask the horses' permission before you started them on this caper?"

"Excuse me, fellow-countrywoman, but if you're really going all those miles you wouldn't catch me coming with you! Not even if you promised to marry me!"

A young overseer at one of the farms, who apparently had the reputation of a wit—his name was Hilario—said to me:

"I suppose you'll be crossing great wide rivers and huge high mountains and facing terrible wild animals, eh? Well, I only know one woman capable of frightening the life out of them."

"Whom do you mean?" I asked.

" My mother-in-law."

I enjoyed the simple fun of those rough fellows who behind it all, since they had all been expert horsemen from their boyhood, could appreciate the task I had set myself and gave me their support in it.

As long as my animals were well looked after and given plenty of food and water I felt the journey was no more than a picnic. My troubles first began when I entered the province of Santiago del Estero, where I was tormented by thirst for days and the heat was suffocating. The problem of water in those sandy wastes and dry deserts plagued me for a long time, though it was not myself so much that I was worrying about, for I found I could generally forget my own needs. My silently suffering horses used to gaze at me imploringly, as if it were in my power to relieve their torture; I could only talk to them encouragingly, trying to make them understand what I was saying and take heart from my words. I knew that the wilderness we were traversing was not an unknown region and that our distress would come to an end some time or other. But before long, when I saw the parched, open mouths of the animals, as they moved slowly forward under the fierce rays of the sun, I began to fear that they would not be able to keep going.

One morning we were crossing one of the driest districts of the province when I saw to my relief a little Indian boy riding towards us on a donkey, with a couple of small earthenware water-jars slung across the animal's forequarters. Neither jar could have contained much more than a gallon. I offered to buy them. He looked at me as though I were asking him for a priceless treasure. I managed to persuade him to sell me the contents of one of the jars, which I poured into a canvas bucket I had with me and after just moistening my lips in the water set it before Principe and Churrito. As they drank they gazed at me with inexpressible gratitude.

I did not yet regard our sufferings as irremediable, for even at the worst moments I was consoled by the reflection that I was in a well-mapped area, inhabited by people who lived there in perfect safety. All the same, the days I spent in Santiago del Estero made me realise that inhospitable country might be more difficult to negotiate than I had hitherto supposed.

I was often to wonder in future, as I had often wondered when I was planning my journey, how the first European invaders found their way about when they were entirely ignorant of the natural features, resources and geographical situation of the lands they were exploring. No maps of such regions existed and they had no information to guide them.

The indomitable explorers of northern Argentina, with Diego de Rojas at their head, had passed through this same desolate country, which was then an utter wilderness. Very few survived the hardships of their struggles with the ferocious climate and the aboriginal inhabitants of the district. History records cases in which the agonies of thirst almost drove the companions of Diego de Rojas out of their minds in the then roadless regions through which I was myself riding.

I crossed the province of Tucumán, which had so astonished the European invaders with the beauty and fertility of its landscape; to-day it is a rich patchwork of sugar plantations, orange groves, flowers and many other products of its lavish soil.

My first encounter with all this glittering natural abundance was at Salta. No traveller ever forgets the forests and majestic peaks that surround the city or the deep gorges, with their driving torrents cleaving the mountains. I will always remember, too, the exquisite valleys, inhabited by the Calchaquies tribe, and the paths between the carob-trees, the poplars and the hawthorn hedges. I can still see the thrilling solitude of the great Cachi, a vast ravine containing only a single village, called Alemania, which is such a quiet, picturesque and lonely little place that one can't imagine how it came to be called 'Germany'.

As I approached Salta on my road northwards, I recalled that the army of Belgrano had been guided through the wild mountain pass of Chachapoyas, while rain fell in torrents, to evade an ambush. The city itself lies buried in exuberant vegetation and is surrounded by mountains. It is no wonder that some call it the 'jewel of the Vale of Lerma'.

I was escorted on my way out of the city by some of the descendants of the famous *gauchos* of Guemes, riding very fine, high-spirited horses, capable of making their way anywhere.

Before I could reach Jujuy, among the impressive foothills of the Andes, Principe suddenly went sick, falling into convulsions. I found that he was suffering from a high fever and there was nothing that I could do for the poor beast. After a few moments he lay motionless, neighing pitifully as he turned his head towards me. With a great deal of effort and affectionate fondling I managed to put him on his legs again, but he was trembling violently and could hardly walk. There was no doubt that the miles we had travelled across rough country in such varying conditions, though they were but the merest hint of what was to come, had undermined his strength.

Luckily his collapse had not occurred in completely open country but in a well-developed area. Major Patino, an expert veterinary surgeon from Jujuy, came providentially to our aid. Treatment of the animal had to be combined with a rest from the journey. There was no suitable place anywhere near so Principe had to be given quarters in a shed which was fitted up as an emergency stable. I remained beside him for three days and watched over him for three nights, calling him by his name, "Principe! Principe!" whenever he moved in his bed of dry straw. It was a grim three days and I thought that they would never end; I was terrified that he would not recover. At the end of three days he recovered.

"No mother could have looked after a son better than you have nursed that animal," the Major told me.

CHAPTER III

ON TO THE HIGHLANDS

WHEN I remounted Principe his eyes gleamed and he held himself proudly; it looked as though he felt nearly as triumphant as I did at the resumption of our expedition. I stroked his neck and caressed him repeatedly, till I noticed that Churrito, my pack-horse, was pulling back, obviously jealous and vexed at my behaviour. I had to dismount, scratch his chest and his haunches and kiss his muzzle before he would consent to regain his normal equanimity. I gave each of them several lumps of sugar which had been presented to me by the owner of a factory near Salta. After that both horses broke into a smart trot, as if eager to bear me on to conquests of fresh territory.

The landscape soon began to assume a different appearance. By the time we had entered the Humahuaca pass it seemed as though we were already in Bolivia. The picturesque ravine ran between mountains of a hundred shades of colour, with tiny villages isolated on their steep flanks, so still that at certain hours they looked quite deserted. At nightfall women came back from the hillsides, their babies on their backs, to houses of sun-dried brick. Little boys accompanied them, wearing diminutive felt hats and driving a few ewes. On a feastday I watched an image of the Virgin being carried in procession. While those who were to take part were assembling, the women, seated on the ground, suckled their infants. Aymara Indians, tall, taciturn men, were coming in from their remote mountain fastnesses to join in the celebrations.

I heard for the first time the melancholy, elegiac notes of the flute, so often in the future to reach my ears across the fells. It is the only sound to be heard in that part of the world until the carnival season comes round and the inhabitants of the pass abandon their calm dignity and give themselves up to frenzied excitement; when the image buried the year before is dug up and the Indians begin to yell and dance incessantly, the flute players accompany the revels. The scenes suggest a barbaric invasion, but they are really only those of boisterous acclamation by people who have passed a whole year in silent labour. This is the land of the aboriginal Omaguaca tribe, which put up a gallant resistance in these hills to the Spanish conquerors.

At La Quiaca, the frontier station on the northern border of Argentina, I stayed a week as a guest of honour; I was a somewhat reluctant guest, as I was held up by Customs formalities and had to spend more time there than I wished. Such complications are sometimes more difficult to elude than a river in flood or the densest jungle.

I took leave of my beautiful native land and soon found myself in a country of low hills and bogs which were just a sample of worse to come. All the same, my horses, though they went slowly, made steady progress. We came eventually to a belt of pasture in which the animals revelled. I took advantage of this to ensure that they ate well, my own hunger being a secondary consideration. Consequently I often went without food and suffered from internal troubles. I could not hesitate in the choice between hurrying on in order to swallow a few mouthfuls myself and allowing my animals all the time they needed to make up for the long hours they had spent on the road without fodder.

For many of the miles I rode through Bolivia I relied for my meals on some dried salt meat that had been given to me. Whenever I reached a relatively cool spot where a certain amount of green vegetation was growing, I would unsaddle the animals and leave them at liberty while I sat down a little way off with my bit of ham. The only trouble was that its salty flavour gave me such a thirst that every stage of the journey passed without finding water became a torment.

After I had left Villazon, one of the first villages on my route through Bolivia, I began to approach Nazareno. By then

27

it was evident from the distant horizons that the landscape
would not vary for a long time to come. Hitherto I had been
climbing ridges, struggling through marshes and leaping
ditches. Now I was faced with nothing but heaps of rock,
with here and there a lonely cactus. Some of these stony
eminences proved terribly rough going. Yet their appearance,
in all the colours of the rainbow, changing their tints every
moment under the light of sun or moon, enchanted me.

At Nazareno I met some travellers who told me they were
countrymen of mine and had come on by mule from the
nearest railway station. They informed me that it would be
impossible to continue my journey by the route I had planned,
adding, with a patronising air:

"Look here, we're from Argentina too and we don't want
you to be let in for what's bound to happen if you insist on
pushing on the way you've begun. Just take the train right
away and put your horses on too. Don't be pig-headed;
no one will ever know which way you came. At any rate
don't take to the road again until you're clear of this devilish
part of the country."

I immediately replied: "I can't do that; or perhaps I
ought to say I don't want to do it. For one thing, I've got
a book here for the local authorities to sign in the places I
pass through or where I stop the night."

At this point they all burst out laughing.

"Moreover," I went on, "I should be ruining my own plans
by doing such a thing. I wouldn't have left home to do a
thing like that. If that had been my intention I should have
gone like other people, as a tourist, without putting my two
poor horses to such a severe test."

"Even though you only cut out the worst part of the
journey?"

"If I only cut out a dozen miles I should always feel guilty
of having failed to stick to my resolve. And one such failure
often leads to another."

"Well, you may be able to go on with your book of signatures. But your horses are going to leave their bones on the
road."

"I'll see to it they don't."

My countrymen continued to urge me to change my mind: "We'll find their shoes, I expect, as we have on other occasions."

I tried to put an end to the conversation by begging them not to take so much trouble over me. They then started making some equivocal jokes about the dangers of a female travelling so many miles all by herself.

I was so accustomed to that sort of teasing wherever I went that it didn't bother me in the slightest. I showed them my gleaming, loaded revolver and the spare cartridges I carried in a leather pouch. Nor did I hesitate to boast that if any of them cared to place a coin on the crown of his hat I could shoot it off cleanly at the first attempt. I knew perfectly well that I wasn't quite such a dead shot as all that. But something seemed to tell me that it wouldn't be a bad idea to put the wind up those boys. Before we parted for the night one of them warned me, with considerable emphasis:

"Anyhow, we shall do all we possibly can to prevent you being so crazy."

After what they had said about the horses probably losing their lives and the persistence with which they had argued about the matter, I was afraid they might intend to do the animals some harm. I went to see the mayor and told him that I would hold him responsible for any future trouble. I said that if anything happened to my horses I should not hesitate to shoot down, there and then, anyone I might suspect of the crime.

The mayor, in his anxiety to prevent any such violent reactions on my part, spent the whole night guarding the horses himself, while I slept near by in hare fashion, keeping one eye open, with a blanket over me. The mayor advised me to get up early and clear out as soon as possible, because, as he put it, there were 'very few attractions in his village'. He said he was a quiet man and didn't want any excitement. He was unlucky on this occasion; as soon as I woke, I uttered a piercing shriek and seized my revolver. The two horses were both bleeding copiously from the withers. I was sure that in spite of all the precautions we had taken they had been injured or tampered with. The mayor was obliged to explain, taking the most solemn oaths that he was telling the truth and going into the matter in the greatest detail before he could convince me, that the wounds had been caused by large vampire bats which very often sucked the blood of animals in that part of the world.

The same thing happened later on more than one occasion during my journey. It was another danger I had to guard against when sleeping in the open air or in stables that could not be properly closed. Bats of this kind abounded in certain districts and were in the habit of hiding among the beams of farm buildings. I remember that once, when both horses had been bitten in this way, Churrito could hardly move all day. As soon as he stood up he would fall down again, owing to the great quantity of blood he had lost.

The impression made upon me by the stern and lonely grandeur of the highlands was no light one, though I should be quite incapable of putting it into words. The interminable panorama of rocks takes on various hues in different conditions of light and at different distances. Sometimes it looks as though made of gold and silver. Vast clouds lower overhead, and as it is difficult to breathe in that oppressive atmosphere progress is inevitably slow and one has no desire to do anything but contemplate at leisure the rolling, desolate hills that shut in every valley. One watches the great masses of rock change colour from red, gold and violet to mauve and blue as twilight falls. At dawn a kaleidoscope of such tints as I should never be able to describe is created by the rising sun.

As I often took short cuts, leaving the road or track, and made my way to places where it had seemed, in the distance, as though there might be good grazing for the animals, I sometimes found myself in very solitary places. There were occasions when I felt I should never see any living thing again except my horses. At such times even those of us who are most devoted to peace and solitude would be glad enough to meet human beings with whom we could exchange even the simplest of greetings.

During the journey across Bolivia, I was riding across one

On the shores of Peru, with my two horses, and the mare Pobre India
which was given to me.

With a family of Peruvian Indians.

With Indians of Ecuador.

Halt with natives of Peru.

of the characteristic stony deserts of the highlands of the country, when I caught sight of an Indian in charge of a flock of llamas. He stared at me, as I rode up to him, in mute amazement. As I came nearer I noticed that the llamas clustered round him were also gazing at me with similar astonishment, stretching their long necks towards me and pricking up their delicately formed ears.

The herdsman came forward to meet me. He was very young, had jet-black hair and wore a short red cloak, much faded. His bare feet, however, which were large and deeply tanned, seemed those of a person considerably older. One of the llamas, which had left the flock to follow him, kept close to his side. She seemed to be his special friend. Her wool, which was white with black patches, looked very clean. Her eyes, large and full, with long lashes, had something womanly about them.

The herdsman addressed me in a mixture of the native dialect and Spanish, begging me to dismount and tell him why I was riding through a desert like that with two horses. As he seemed a decent young fellow I told him that I should be glad enough of a good long rest if he could show me a place with plenty of good grazing and water for the animals. Soon we were seated among the rocks of a slope where some tough but eatable grass was growing, with a clear brook running about a hundred yards away. I gave him a brief explanation of my presence. He showed much interest in my clothing and the trappings of the horses, touching them with childlike curiosity. It was clear enough that he had very little idea what I was talking about. That didn't surprise me in a little Indian boy, for very few people seemed to understand why anyone should take so much trouble for no immediate or practical purpose.

After a while the lad, who seemed to have fallen into a doze, woke up and said that if I liked we could go and get some very valuable bracelets and other trinkets, goldsmiths' and silversmiths' work, which he had hidden. We should then both be rich, he said, and be able to travel to countries very far away, 'quite 150 miles off', as he put it.

I listened dreamily, as though to a fairy-tale, for our surroundings encouraged the play of fantasy. When I asked him how he could think of leaving his flock he answered confidently that there were plenty of other boys like himself about, who would come and take his place the very next day. I then suggested that the police or other authorities might meet us on the road and confiscate all his bracelets and other valuables. But that didn't worry him.

"I know mountain paths," he said, "where such people as you mention could never find us."

I knew that the local craftsmen were skilled in the working of gold and silver; they could produce positive masterpieces in that line. But everything the boy said sounded to me like some fancy of his own, invented in his long hours of solitude and stimulated by a longing for adventure of which he himself was scarcely aware. I pointed out that I could not let him ride the other horse, as I needed it for my baggage. Thereupon he burst into hearty laughter, saying he had never dreamed of such a thing. He would be able to keep up on foot with the animals, he told me, and they would tire before he did.

This was perfectly true. The natives of those parts can move at a tireless trot, slow or fast, just like horses. And in this particular case, actually, the boy would make better progress, for my horses were suffering to a certain extent from the rarification of the air. Fatigue was gaining steadily upon them and I was obliged to rest them more and more often.

The ground was becoming still more difficult to traverse. Broad streams and rivers were flowing down the sides of the mountains, crossing and running into one another, so that it was hard to decide which way to go.

I don't know whether my little Indian would really have been able to find secret paths through the mazes of the highlands. It was a fact, however, that I should not be able to make any further headway in those parts without some idea at least of where I was going. Accordingly I stopped at the first group of huts I came to and asked the headman for a guide. I obtained one, but he accompanied me with rather a bad grace.

I repeated these tactics between Suipacha, a village which

played a certain part in the revolutionary wars of South America, and Tupiza, the next town along my route. On the latter occasion the headman picked out a lusty young fellow who was most reluctant to obey his orders and argued with him for quite a time. So far as I could make out his objection seemed to be that since he knew the passes very well he also knew that they were extremely difficult to negotiate. Turning to myself, he also warned me that the river currents were very capricious and difficult to deal with in a crossing. The marshes, too, were a real danger, he added, especially to such heavily laden animals. However, I was determined to go on whatever he might say. I told him this and insisted, moreover, that he was always to go ahead of me, never behind or at my side. I had good reason to stick to that rule in future, whenever I employed a guide of any sort. To make assurance doubly sure I invariably kept my revolver handy.

I should say here that the native inhabitants of these extensive tracts of country generally respect a traveller's property and person. As a rule, in fact, they take no interest whatever in either. Usually a guide's sole preoccupation is to have done with the road and its perils as soon as possible and regain the tranquillity of his village or his farm.

On the present occasion my guide rode ahead of me on a mule. However good a walker he might be it was impossible to negotiate those stony and muddy waters on foot. The task required very great care and skill. He often reined in the mule and sat still for a while, thinking over what his next step should be.

All of a sudden he pulled up in decided fashion. "We've arrived. You won't need me any more now."

I pointed out that the devilish track we were following was not changing for the better but on the contrary for the worse. Nevertheless, he insisted that he had done all he had been asked to do. I was obliged to address him in pretty strong language and warn him that he would regret it if he did not at least guide me to some point from which the next village would be visible.

I had to ford with the same guide a very wide and muddy river. We were both aware that there was a distinct risk of not reaching the opposite bank. But we both in the end succeeded in doing so.

After skirting a high ridge and following a switchback path that seemed interminable I eventually came to a plantation house where I was able to rest and recuperate for a while from my labours. The crops grown on the estate were few but flourishing. I was welcomed by the lady who owned the plantation and her daughter, a very young girl, riding a white horse. They both expressed great admiration for my project and even encouraged me to proceed with it. But they warned me that before doing so I had better think it over again very carefully, if what they saw were all the resources I had at my disposal.

The next morning I set off once more on my journey, without allowing myself to be put off by their slightly gloomy forecast of the difficulties ahead.

The daughter of the house offered to ride a good part of the way with me in order to show me how best to avoid being caught in the maze of rivers. She accompanied me on her white horse, with one of the male farm-servants riding pillion behind her.

It was the season in which torrents flowed down from the mountains and the rock-strewn ground was flooded with streams running in all directions, some of them being very wide and deep. As a rule we could only cross them with the water coming up to the horses' chests or by making the animals swim.

My journey very nearly came to an end in one of those rivers, which I had not thought was so deep; it would have been a pity, at such an early stage of the ride. I was mounted on Principe, whose turn it was that day. I rode the horses turn and turn about, so that the one I rode would serve as a pack-horse the following day, carrying a load of baggage weighing some eighty pounds.

The current was very strong. It dragged the animals out of their course and they struggled wildly in their efforts to swim on. The situation became alarming when I noticed that Principe was being swept away downstream and making no progress across at all. It seemed impossible for us ever to reach the opposite bank. I began to fear that the current would prove too much for the horses. At last it started to spin Principe round like a helpless plaything. A wave swept me from the saddle and I thought my last moment had come. I managed to catch hold of one of the stirrups at the very moment when the mad rush of waters seemed about to overwhelm me and I succeeded in getting my head above water.

My fingers were gripping so hard that the pain almost forced me to loosen them. By this time I could see neither the horses nor any fixed object anywhere near me. Suddenly, with a supreme effort, my heroic Principe managed to come out of his spin and began swimming diagonally towards the bank we had just left. After a frantic struggle, in which I tugged at the pack-horse and the other horse tugged at me, for I was still unconsciously digging my fingers into his stirrup, the three of us reached the bank. I was very near to fainting and would probably still have been carried away by the flood if some labourers who were setting up a snare for game with wooden posts had not waded breast high into the river and pulled me and the animals out.

When I had recovered my faculties to some extent the men asked:

"Couldn't you see for yourself that the river is impassable?"

"What is one to do, then, if it's in one's way?"

"You either build a raft or wait for the dry season."

There was, of course, an alternative solution which would be to follow the bank until one found a place where the river was running lower, although this might mean going some miles out of one's way.

In the end we managed to ford the river. But on the other side I found a stretch of rocks and marsh that was exceedingly difficult to negotiate.

Fortunately, it was not the season of intense cold—that was awaiting me elsewhere—for in this part of the country when the temperature falls to its lowest donkeys and other animals are often frozen to death.

It is astonishing that the Indian inhabitants of these regions can stand such extreme degrees of cold and live on a soil that affords so very little nourishment. They themselves attribute their powers of endurance to the leaves of the coca plant, which they are always chewing and carry about with them in a leather pouch. They often praised the qualities of this leaf to me and advised me to chew it as a stimulant which would enable me to endure all the hardships of my journey. I had always supposed that the secret of its effect was the production of a state of insensibility which might give rise to an artificial type of energy. I must confess, however, that at times I did decide to resort to it when I felt that I had reached the limit of my strength, and on those occasions the coca leaf duly did the trick for me.

I arrived, almost without drawing rein, though my temples were humming with the strain, at the town of Tupiza in the province of Sud Chichas. I devoted the last remnant of my strength to checking the condition of the animals and of my baggage. I spread out everything that was wet to dry and made a careful examination of the waterproof covers of my road-book and other documents. Then I dropped on my bed in the delirium of a fever which kept me there for three days.

I owe a debt of gratitude to Dr. Exposito, a physician in the service of the Oploca Company, of which I shall also have occasion to make grateful mention in the pages which follow. I was given a cordial send-off. The entire population turned out to see me start. I noticed in particular great numbers of half-breed women, wearing their distinctive white hats, stiff as the hardest cardboard and very high in the crown, and the inevitable two long tresses of hair as well as the many short, hooped petticoats, one on top of another.

Chapter IV

A NIGHT OF TERROR

THE rest had done the animals good, but they still suffered from the biting of bats, which had started again. I decided to cover them up at night with blankets. Their health was improving and gave me no cause for anxiety; I was sure that if they had a relapse it would not be because I had failed to give them all the attention they required.

Those who take horses with them on such a journey as mine must never neglect the hundred and one details that the care of the animals involves. Their backs have to be regularly examined for sores made by the saddle. If these are allowed to fester there will be no getting rid of them throughout the journey. Hoofs have to be well looked after and kept properly greased. On hot days the animals should be allowed to bathe in any water that may be met with. If there is much wind about when they are unsaddled the greatest care must be taken to cover them with blankets to prevent them catching cold or pneumonia. Girths should always be slackened when traversing fairly smooth ground, if there is no need to hurry. Someone once tightened the girths of one of my horses without my noticing it and caused swellings which lasted three or four days. In short, animals which have to endure the fatigues of a long journey have to be kept fit, and they require considerable attention.

I proceeded to ride the ten miles from Tupiza to Oploca. At the latter place the good angels who watch over the needs of persevering travellers took the forms of Señor Caballero, the manager of the Railway Company, Captain Mendez, and other employees of this company. They offered to do their best to solve one of the fundamental problems I had to deal with: that of feeding the horses. Orders were given to all the railway stations on my route to lay in adequate stocks of alfalfa (lucerne) as fodder for my animals. The company happened to grow it and could supply any amount.

Nevertheless, this step did not wholly meet my difficulty, as I should be taking short cuts across country and might not be able to find my way at the proper time to the railway stations in question.

Some twenty-five miles further on I reached Oro Ingenio, which is well over 10,000 feet above sea-level, and the height began to have its usual effect on all three of us.

While I was riding out of the town a terrific rainstorm overtook me; it did not really take me by surprise, for at that period rain was falling almost every day. I felt its lasting effects for quite half the time I spent in Bolivia, and used to arrive drenched at practically every place where I intended to stay overnight. The rain often turned to hail, the violent shower of stones bringing the horses to a standstill, for the poor things cannot close their eyes as we do and are obliged to turn their backs to the onslaught.

On leaving Oro Ingenio I decided, in order to avoid a detour of several miles, to ride along a certain canyon or deep gorge, not far from the railway station at Chorro.

The gorge looked rather formidable, but I thought I could make my way through it. It was a narrow ravine with perpendicular walls like the sides of huge buildings. A small stream, shallow enough for the horses, ran along the bottom of it.

Everyone warned me that I should be very frightened in that canyon; they had all made a special point of adding: "Mind the *angosto* doesn't catch you. Otherwise you'll be done for."

By the *angosto* they meant both the wind and the sudden rise, due to rain, of the waters in the ravine, which added to the changes of the ravine itself. It was common local knowledge that if rain fell heavily enough to produce such a rise there would be not much hope of leaving the ravine alive. I did not see, however, how anything out of the way could happen during the time I should take to ride from one point of refuge to another.

Nevertheless, the worst happened. It began to rain very hard. Principe, moreover, even before it began to rain, had been showing distinct signs of not wanting to go on. For the first and last time I had to use every resource at my disposal, even the whip, for all I was worth, to get him to move. As we shall see, the horse was perfectly right. Shortly afterwards the water began to rise all along the ravine. An hour later the animals could hardly take a single step. The wind roared between the sheer walls of the gorge and the sky above our heads had turned black. I realised the danger and made a supreme effort to retain my self-control.

Should I continue to press on and take the risk of exhausting the horses in the hope of emerging from the ravine or should I turn back and go out the way I had come in? I didn't know which to do and began to feel frightened. All the tales I had heard of the *angosto* and its victims rang in my ears. Night was coming on and it seemed to me that I had lost all sense of direction. I continued in this state of confusion until about nine in the evening. Then I decided to turn back, though I had no very certain knowledge which would be the way back and which the way forward. In any case the horses were incapable of proceeding in either direction. They were repeatedly struck by the swirling current and the stones it dragged along. They snorted and panted, their flanks heaving. It was impossible to force them to move a step.

My only chance appeared to be to try to find, though it was almost pitch dark, some place where I might manage to scramble cat-like up the rugged face of the cliff and reach the heights. I don't quite know how we did it, though it was probably because the animals were as frantic as myself, but we did at last succeed in clambering out of the ravine up that mighty wall of rock. Almost fainting, I let myself fall on a boulder, beside my equally lost and exhausted companions. I felt quite overwhelmed by loneliness and despair. Occasionally the moon showed dimly through a wind-torn rent in the clouds, illuminating all round me the most desolate landscape imaginable, with hardly a single shrub growing in the waste of rocks. I believe that the terror of that vigil, in a situation that could not very well be worse, was increased by the accumulated fears from which I had suffered ever since the beginning of my journey. I lost all my habitual self-possession and felt like a panic-stricken little girl. I couldn't control my reflexes. Sometimes I tried to scream without being able to. Sometimes I yelled at the top of my voice. Suddenly I started singing wildly, to take my mind off my predicament. The night seemed to last for ever. Whenever the clouds overhead gathered and thickened, my dread increased, for I knew this meant the rain would fall faster.

At last it began to grow light and the shapes of the mountains became visible. I recovered my equanimity to a certain extent, though I still had to find out which way to go. I hadn't the faintest idea where I was.

I finally decided to mount and let the horse take me wherever it felt inclined. These tactics generally succeed, and the present occasion was no exception. I eventually found myself riding along a rough track.

As the day brightened the wet rocks after the night of rain gleamed red, yellow and blue in the rays of the sun. Four peasants who were walking along a slope some distance away noticed us. They approached with every sign of astonishment, amazed at the way I was dressed and above all at my being a woman. They stared at my baggy trousers, my riding-boots and my long yellow hair as if they were encountering a wild beast they had never even heard of in all their lives.

I was quite used to surprised expressions of this sort, which did not as a rule hold up my progress. I had aroused a great deal of wonder and comment in a certain mining district on my route, where I was nevertheless put up for the night in one of the office buildings belonging to Patino, the tin king. At that time I had just crossed some ten miles of the most desolate country I have ever seen. There was not a tree, not a bush, not even an anthill. The landscape was thoroughly typical of the mineral regions of those parts.

The four peasants guided me to a place called Tres Palcas,

where I found a post-office but, alas, nothing to eat. Such things are always happening on a journey of this kind. A certain requirement arises, you find a way of dealing with it and then another takes its place. All three of us were famished. And as usual I suffered more from the horses' pangs of hunger than from my own. So far as I was concerned I was satisfied with some maize offered me by a number of the Indian women, who each held out a fistful towards me. They gave me the only food they had, maize being the mainstay of their diet. As for the horses, Captain Mendez, whom I have already mentioned, came to their rescue. On receipt of a telegram from me announcing my predicament he forwarded a consignment of alfalfa by rail from Tupiza.

As I was leaving Tres Palcas a violent hailstorm drove me back. The horses were trembling with the cold, which grew more biting every moment. Their condition worried me and I took them with me into a room I had been given to sleep in. I kept them near my bed, where I could listen to their breathing, for I was afraid one or both of them might have caught pneumonia. It was touching to see their gratitude for my maternal care; of their own accord they turned their hind legs away from me in case they should inconvenience me in any way and put their heads as near as they could to my own. As soon as I had fed them I gave them my blankets, preferring to sleep with a light covering. I ate a mouthful of fried bread and potatoes which the kindhearted Indian women brought me.

When we resumed our journey I noticed that it was getting colder and colder. We were now approaching Escoriani, some 13,000 feet above sea-level. Cold was destined to be one of my chief enemies almost all the time I was in Bolivia. It was particularly piercing in the district called The Plateau. On several occasions my lips swelled and hardened to such an extent that I was unable to eat. Consequently, in addition to the external chill of the atmosphere, I was afflicted no less by internal chills.

The road now before me led into further deep gorges resembling that of the *Angosto* of evil memory. I came to the conclusion, after my experiences there, that I should never be able to get through the ravines without a guide to accompany me.

We travelled along the river-beds, as there was no proper track. At times I imagined we were being stoned by people on the mountainsides. The fact was, however, that at certain points continuous avalanches of rocks fell regularly. The guides showed me how to guard against this fresh danger. They thus satisfactorily carried out one part of their duties. But their other duty, that of accompanying me as far as my destination, they only fulfilled in a very sketchy manner. They constantly left me and were replaced by others, for, although they were natives of the locality, they seemed to suffer a good deal from the bad weather and the rough going. At the approaches to Escoriani the storms of hail so afflicted the horses that it became necessary to call a halt and place them under cover in a coal-shed belonging to a small railway station.

The place could hardly be called a village. It consisted only of a few scattered huts occupied by Indians and a military post.

Between this hamlet, called Uyuni, and Chita, thirty miles further on, I had to cross an exceedingly unpleasant tract of marshland, into which the hoofs of the horses sank so deeply that I was obliged to dismount to extract them, running the risk of being stuck just as fast myself. In one village the people told me that I ought to mark the way I went with such objects as pieces of cloth or notched sticks, to blaze my trail, as they might very easily be ordered to go in search of me if I got lost, which was highly probable.

CHAPTER V

LOCAL CHIEFTAINS

I WAS not enthusiastic about marking my path in the way suggested, for it seemed to me that if I did do this whenever I reached regions where it was difficult to find the way I should spend practically the whole of my time cutting up cloth and breaking off pieces of wood. But I did see the villagers' point; it was almost impossible to be sure of one's direction among those endless swamps. There appeared to be no end to them. I had to make a great effort not to give way to despair and renounce all hope of further progress.

Nevertheless, I did go on and got absolutely lost somewhere near Chita. The inhabitants had heard of my approach and came out to look for me in a great state of excitement and wonder. The mayor himself, followed by a large number of Indians, frantically searched the marshes, waving a lantern with the object of attracting my attention. At intervals the whole party shouted in chorus, their yells drowning the tumult of the storm. Forked lightning was darting through the sky; one of the flashes so dazzled Principe that he reared in his fright and I had a good deal of trouble in preventing him from bolting.

At last the mayor and his companions, to their great relief, tracked me down among the swamps. They escorted me in triumph to their rude huts, where I got a shake-down for the night.

On my taking the road for Rio Mulato, thirty-five miles from Chita, I was met by a combined sand and hail storm which would have stopped a regiment. The speed of the wind was such that the fine grains of sand pelted me like bullets from a machine-gun, while volleys of hailstones struck me like projectiles. I

43

took refuge at a farm occupied by Indians who, as usual, received me with characteristic hospitality, taciturn but courteous. I had already learnt and continued thereafter to adopt their custom of only uttering the most indispensable phrases and their special form of politeness, which consists in showing signs of enjoying the meals offered and the simple attentions bestowed on a guest and in imitating the gestures and attitudes of one's hosts. I pretended to be greatly delighted with their flour-cakes and the seductive melancholy of their pipe-music. On such occasions the old men, or the most important of the women who were entertaining me, would smile and ask: "Won't you stay over to-morrow, Missie?" or "Missie, shall we get something for your horses to eat?"

On this stage, and for a good deal of my journey, I very often slept in the most extraordinary places, lonely post-offices, stone buildings which had fallen into ruin and deserted hovels, but I liked best of all to stay at an Indian farm. As a rule, under the pretext that it was necessary to remain with the horses, I slept out of doors, unless the cold was really frightful, for the congestion indoors rendered the air there intolerably oppressive. Almost always the headman would order a couple of the male residents to keep watch all night over my animals, mainly to prevent their being stolen. Indifference to proximity of the sexes was normal in such places and when I tried to avoid it I met with surprise or incomprehension. At the farm where I now was my hosts threw a few sheepskins down in the open for me to sleep on. A young man of twenty-four came to sleep on the one next to mine, which was beside the horses. I told the older people in the house that I should prefer an elderly couple as my neighbours for the night. The woman I spoke to did not seem to understand.

"Why don't you want the boy to sleep there?" she asked.

Obviously she had put the question in all innocence. I did not, therefore, explain the reason for my request, but merely insisted upon it. It is a fact that proximity does not imply any looseness of morals among any but a very few of the rural communities of Indians or native populations in any of the countries I have visited. At any rate nothing of the kind is to be observed even in the poorest or most primitive districts, where the women go about bare-breasted. Nor does one notice, as one does among the white races, what amounts to an obsession with that kind of thing.

In any case the nights I spent surrounded by other people were more restful and less disturbed by bad dreams than my lonely ones. I used to dream, especially if I were sleeping in solitary places, about all my past adventures, with their horrors exaggerated and rendered even more terrifying. Sometimes I used to wake up struggling and screaming; I was glad I had more control over myself when I was awake!

While on the subject of these little Indian villages, I am reminded of an adventure that occurred to me one day during my wanderings. A certain man, whose christian names were Pedro Juan, was a widower, though still comparatively young. He paid a great deal of attention to me in every way, so much so that I stayed a day longer in his village than I had intended. He picked ten men to keep watch over the horses at night. Such a large body of protectors made me somewhat uneasy and I must confess that I suspected a plot; but it did not turn out that way. So that I might sleep under a roof without being disturbed Pedro Juan moved out of his own dwelling, little more than a hut, where eight or ten persons normally slept, and passed the night out of doors. It was freezing that night as I well remember. While I was getting ready to saddle up and leave, he begged for a few words alone with me. As a matter of fact we did not talk alone; a few old women, apparently as indifferent as so many embalmed corpses, were present—presumably to ensure that our conversation did not take place without witnesses.

With scarcely any preparatory beating about the bush the man bluntly proposed that I should remain in the village and share in all the wealth and privileges he enjoyed as chief. He did in fact own a certain amount of very inferior land and a flock of llamas larger than those of a number of his neighbours put together. He also had some women and boys working for him at the picturesque local loom, where they made cloaks and other garments, beautifully coloured and embroidered.

I thought he was making one of those jokes so often played upon travellers and not meant to be taken seriously. So without any sign of annoyance or rejecting his proposal out of hand, I asked:

"Are you suggesting, then, that we should marry?"

He replied that this was just what he did mean, adding that close by, at a distance of some thirty miles, there was a church where a priest officiated from time to time for such purposes. All I would have to do would be to agree to his suggestion and kneel down with him for a few minutes.

From my knowledge of the character and habits of Indians I was aware that a proposal of this kind was very seldom made. Either because such a plan would be regarded as impracticable or else because white women do not attract Indians, they rarely pay court to females of the so-called white-skinned races.

The chief had dressed for this interview in his best holiday attire, which was very brightly coloured. He wore his best hat and carried a showy staff. I marvelled at the earnest and unaffected way in which he pressed his suit. He may have supposed that this part of the world consisted entirely of poverty-stricken and sleepy villages little better equipped than his own and that consequently it could not matter much to anyone whether one of them was chosen rather than another.

But I really don't know what he did think or why he thought it. What I do know is that I found it difficult to make him understand the excuses I made and the reasons why the 'fair-haired missie' could not accept his proposal. He would not even listen to what I said about the impossibility of interrupting my journey, now that it had been given official sanction by the signatures and stamps of the municipal authorities in my book. Limiting the whole question to the conditions prevailing in his own district, he told me that he too had sometimes undertaken a journey into the distant hills with his llamas, but had soon decided to cut it short before any serious trouble arose. I was reduced to informing him, in a solemn whisper, that I was under Government orders "in connection with the relations between Canada and Argentina, you know." He knew very little, in fact, about either country. And as his ideas about nations, governments and their orders were somewhat vague, he continued to urge me to comply with his wishes. I began to laugh. But soon the gravity of his expression made me stop. I resorted to evasive tactics, pointing out that I could not disobey my Government.

"Orders are orders," I said. "But on my return I shall be coming back this way and then we can reconsider the matter, though I expect that by then you will have married one of the pretty girls I have seen round about here."

I may as well confess here that I often used the phrase, 'We'll talk it over when I return', though I knew perfectly well that I should never retrace my steps. I used it on a number of different occasions, but nearly always in the case of so-called 'civilised' men, hardly ever among Indians, peasants or shepherds. I have no particularly disagreeable recollection of such incidents, regarding them as merely so many polite attentions. A police-sergeant or a farmer or a fellow hotel-resident or whoever it might be—their professions don't matter—would suggest that I might break off my journey for 'sentimental' reasons and then I would use that 'when I return' phrase. These were cases for the most part of a 'passing fancy' which would pass as I did myself. They were largely inspired by the uncommon nature of my undertaking. On the few occasions of a different kind, when violence and criminal intentions were in view, I invariably relied on taking the necessary action at the right moment, as well as on my revolver or rifle.

In the case of the worthy Pedro Juan, however, I was at my wit's end to think of some expedient to put him off. He spoke to the old women present, who proceeded to overwhelm me with flattering compliments. It occurred to me that there was a risk of the chief's scheme of a marriage with me being made public. Accordingly, that night I saddled and groomed the horses. As soon as everyone was asleep I secretly led them out a good distance from the farm buildings, then mounted and rode off at a gallop. It was very rude of me, I admit, to make off like that, but I couldn't think of anything else to do.

I spent New Year's Day, 1951, at Rio Mulato, 12,500 feet above sea-level. I was entertained throughout the night by the customary festivities, in which both Indians and non-Indians took part. I had to drink quantities of the brandy passed round by the revellers though I was careful not to take too much and poured away the contents of my glass when an opportunity offered.

Next day the chief, a man of about fifty, with a benevolent cast of countenance, told me—and I thoroughly agreed with him—that the country I should now have to cross would be impassable unless I took a guide with me who knew the fords. He boasted that he himself was perhaps the one man in the entire district who could be trusted not to make any mistake in the matter. As soon as I realised that the fumes of what he had drunk the night before had passed off, I resolved to take advantage of his offer and rely upon his knowledge of the region. Two boys also volunteered to accompany me as guides. But the chief dismissed them with a contemptuous smile.

"They don't know anything," he said. "They ought to be still sucking their mothers' breasts."

He himself set off with great confidence, with the air of a man about to travel round the world. I had given him a half promise that if he got too tired I might allow him to ride the pack-horse and he had answered that he would never dream of riding such an animal. These people never ride even a donkey. The only quadruped they make use of is the llama, very common in this part of the country; when they adopt their characteristic trot they can cover as much ground, or even more, within the same period, as a horse or a mule.

At first the dashing chieftain strode along with much pomp and showed a good deal of skill in finding the necessary intricate paths through that incessant maze of streams and torrents. But the task grew more and more difficult. Soon I could see that he was beginning gradually to lose heart.

When we reached a small village I had not expected to come across in such a wilderness the bombastic swagger of my expert was punctured for good.

"Now you'll be able to go ahead quite well, Missie. As you see, I've now done all I can for you."

"But this is just the very worst part of it!"

"Oh no. In a few minutes you'll find it's perfectly all right."

I almost invariably had this experience with the natives who volunteered to guide me. They all showed great enthusiasm to begin with. But the further they left their valleys or farms behind the more rapidly the irresistible desire to return took possession of them.

The consequence in this case was that I found myself abandoned by the chief at the very moment I was plunging into the heart of a mountainous zone even more formidable than the one before. All the sand and rocks in the world seemed to have piled themselves up there in order to strangle the growth of any tree or green thing at birth. I must confess that I could not allow myself the luxury of concentrating upon the beauty or otherwise of the landscape rather than on its practical consequences. Lack of variety in any tract of country tends to make the traveller lose his bearings, since no landmarks exist to which he can refer. And the absence of any vegetation to rejoice the eye also meant that there would be no grazing for the horses.

Both these fears were realized; I was lost in the desert and had nothing to fill any of our three mouths. It was true that there was plenty of water, only too much. That day was another very painful one and I wept bitterly over the pitiable state of my animals. It was not the first or last time I did so. But I never cried except when I was utterly alone, with no one to see me. If I never emerged, I thought, from that freezing and wind-swept desert of sand and rock, my horses would perish miserably. I could see neither the smoke of any hut nor even the distant forms of a few llamas. I dropped to the ground, in the shelter of a rock, without letting go of the reins of my two companions. I would have been glad to see a lizard scurry past or a mouse frisk by or any sign of life to relieve the monotony of that desolate waste. I asked myself, in profound discouragement, whether it was due to any excessive stupidity of my own that I had lost my way so often.

I did as I had done in previous cases of the kind. Without making up my mind I mounted, let the reins lie loose and told my horses: "You know best which way to go."

My horse, performing prodigies of detection, as he cocked his ears north, south, east and west, went in the direction where, after all, I might have expected him to go. He returned to the last village on our route. When the mayor—even the smallest hamlet possesses one—saw us, he raised his hands to his head to show how shocked he was at the state in which we had returned. I was bending low in the saddle, half fainting with hunger and altogether in a most pitiable condition.

The chief who had recently been with me had said to the mayor: "I've just left that woman who is going round the world on horseback after telling her all about the road. If she comes back it can only be that she's tired of travelling round the world and wants to rest."

I explained to the mayor: "It was he who got tired, tired of showing me the way. His courage failed him too soon."

At this remark the mayor flew into a passion and gave a display of his authority. He blew a terrific blast on his silver whistle. More than two hundred Indians ran up from all directions and assembled round us.

The mayor commanded silence and addressed the meeting in highflown style.

"This gallant woman has come with her two horses from a beautiful country of the same family as our own. It is very rich and very big and is called Argentina. She is going to another country, further from here than La Paz, a hundred times further in fact, and now she is passing through our country. She is under a duty and obligation, which she feels to be sacred, to finish her journey. The ground she has come up against in these parts is, as you know, extremely difficult to travel over. She needs a guide who knows the district to accompany her. Is there any brave man here who would like to go with her, even if it's only as far as Sevaruyo?''

A short silence ensued. I heard Churrito neigh, as though he too would like to hear the answer.

A tall young Indian stepped forward. All eyes were fixed upon him, even those of the women, who had discreetly gathered a short distance away.

"I will accompany her," he said.

The mayor, looking very pleased, congratulated him, casting a triumphant glance at me, as much as to say: 'The people in my village are ready for anything!'

When I saw the young man stride off resolutely to fetch his pouch with the coca-leaves and few other little things he needed, then seize the reins of my hourse and start off along the road as if he really meant business, I said to myself: "Well, now at last I have someone who won't run away!"

We soon left the village behind and found ourselves, for the rest of that day, climbing and scrambling up steep, winding paths of typical highland character, a perfect torment for the horses. They had to be rested every few yards. It was a miracle how they kept their balance on the ridges, their hoofs slipping again and again, while their iron shoes struck sparks from the flint. My own feet recoiled from the razor-edged rocks that cut and tore at the leather of my boots. Suddenly, Churrito lost his footing, slipped and gave vent to a piteous neigh. Luckily both I myself and the guide were holding on with all our strength to the reins. After frantic efforts we regained control of him, enabling him to pull himself together and stand up. All three of us then rested from our labours for a while, standing on a ledge so narrow that we could scarcely move.

After a time I acquired a certain dexterity in this mode of progress, the unhappy animals climbing with their hoofs and we on hands and knees, occasionally hanging on by our very finger-tips. All the same, whenever I had to face this exasperating task afresh, it seemed to me that the last time I had done it had been easier. It was an ordeal involving strain on eyes, limbs and nerves. I held my breath to see how the horses suffered under this cruel test of their powers of endurance and their spirit.

Sometimes it was necessary to drop the reins and go ahead of the animals. But when they took it into their heads to go first, they proceeded by leaps and bounds which endangered our position as we climbed upright or on all fours, whichever seemed best. At such times I had to mount and pray to heaven that the beast wouldn't slip. If it did, it was not going to bother much about its rider. To all these worries were added, in my own case, the effects of the altitude, which I felt in the throbbing of my heart and temples. The guide did not appear to suffer in this way. He chewed steadily, without uttering a word, at his coca-leaf. But I could read increasing terror in his features.

In scrambling up a steep gradient one of the horses, trying to find a foothold, jostled the other; both stumbled and fell. I raised my hands to my head, screamed and covered my eyes. I was still trembling with fright when I breathed again. The horses had managed to save themselves from rolling down the precipice. With frantic efforts, after wild pawing with their hoofs, they first knelt, then regained their feet.

The Indian's terror increased in proportion to the difficulties of the ascent. I was in no state, myself, to make prolonged reflections. But I could not help thinking: 'Here's another one who's going to let me down.' His face plainly showed his discouragement, although when we started out he had more than once declared that he was ready to accompany me wherever I went, even if it were to the end of the world. Well, we hadn't got to the end of the world yet, though we had got to the end of all territory into which human or equine beings could reasonably be expected to penetrate. The rugged horizon held out no hope of anything but a continuation of the vindictive hostility of nature. Finally the young guide came to a halt in front of the horses. He turned to me and announced —as resolutely as he had proclaimed his heroic intentions in the village—

"I'm not going any further."

I yelled at him with all the power of my lungs: "I'm not going to let you be the third to desert me!"

He had no idea what I meant nor would he have cared in the slightest whether he would be the third or the first of a series he knew nothing whatever about. But my recollection of former guides who had left me in the lurch, to be lost at the most critical point of the day's journey, had naturally made me furious.

As he refused to listen to me I covered him with my revolver and told him he would have to put up with the consequences.

He immediately ran off in a rather childish fashion and hid in a cluster of jujube trees. I pursued him, flourishing my weapon. The man was young and very powerfully built. If it had come to a hand-to-hand struggle I should not have been able to master him. Obviously, should he defy me to shoot, I could never make up my mind to press the trigger and kill him.

Fortunately, no one can ever guess what someone else is thinking. In the end my threats proved sufficient and he muttered: "All right then. Let's go on."

A moment later he added: "Come on, Missie. We'll walk side by side."

"Not if I know it!" I shouted back at him. "You go ahead and stay there! Guides and people I don't know always have to walk in front of me!"

I had my way and we continued our journey accordingly. From time to time the young man turned his head, regarding me with an expression which seemed to say: " Don't you see how senseless it is to go on with a climb like this?"

Logically, he was right; but not even logic can stand in the way when the whole of one's will-power is concentrated on carrying out a plan. Rain began to fall with increasing violence. The horses had to keep their heads between their legs. I laid my own head close to the neck of the horse I was riding. The Indian crawled on all fours nearly all the time and I never let him out of my sight. In this fashion, creeping along like damned souls, the horses almost at their last gasp, we covered the twenty-five miles or so to Sevaruyo.

In the village the greatest festival of the year was taking place. I should have preferred to arrive on a quiet occasion, when it would be easier to avoid revellers. Everyone we met seemed to be drunk. It was as though some kind of madness had suddenly attacked a peaceful and normally conventional population. The streets were filled with people singing, dancing and yelling uninterruptedly. The groups I accosted were all either shrieking or weeping and it seemed impossible to find anybody who might show me where a modest lodging for the night could be obtained.

My arrival, however, made a great impression on the intoxicated crowds. Some made attempts to seize me, others came to my rescue. I was the centre of so riotous a mob that I was afraid of being knocked over every moment. Occasionally I spurred my horse to frighten and scatter the most importunate. I had to make the most energetic efforts, forcing the horses into the crowd and threatening individuals with my whip. Eventually, the whole village having been made aware of my presence, a large number of wildly gesticulating women arrived and carried me off, in the attempt to settle my problem, to the stationmaster. But at the railway station everyone was hopelessly drunk. I took refuge in the house of a telegraph-office employee, whose family allowed me to remain, as they did not seem to be quite so far gone in liquor as the rest.

The infernal tumult in the streets rose to a climax, for the strangeness of the figure I cut in that village had redoubled the frenzy of the festivities.

A group of musicians, all so drunk that they kept falling down and getting up again, came to offer me a noisy serenade. Eventually they carted me off in a triumphal procession through the streets.

One of the Indians, taking advantage of the confusion, climbed on to Churrito's back. As he had no idea how to ride and the animal had already been frightened by the uproar and our perpetual dodging about from one place to another, the horse took the bit in his teeth and bolted, with the intoxicated native clinging for all he was worth to the saddle.

I gave chase, at a gallop, on Principe. The yelling of the Indians became frantic, all screaming at the tops of their voices that the devil himself had entered into the body of the horse that had bolted. The implication was that if one of my horses could be possessed by Satan I could not be very far from demoniac possession myself.

As ill-luck would have it, Churrito knocked down some unfortunate woman and also upset the roof of a shrine containing an image, the name of which I can't remember, prominently concerned in the festivities. The result was that when I reached Churrito and managed to calm him down by repeatedly calling his name I found myself surrounded by a crowd that looked really ugly. I gathered, in particular, from their outcries, that they intended to do the 'possessed' Churrito some serious mischief.

I called out that I was only the advanced guard of a whole army of riders like myself, which would arrive very soon, with much bigger devils in their horses, and that they would not leave the humblest villager with a head on his shoulders. I could hardly make myself heard above the tumult. But a few old women understood what I was saying and immediately dashed off with loud shrieks, spreading the news in all directions.

This incident caused a certain mitigation in the fury of the mob. I took advantage of it to make my escape, as fast as my two horses could gallop. The Indians did not pursue me. I felt sure they were in such a state of senseless bewilderment that a few hours later they would probably be unable to recall the details of what had happened.

The excitement and danger had so exhausted me that I slept out of doors that night. It was very cold and my breathing had been so much affected by the altitude that I woke up the next morning with chattering teeth and the characteristic 'whistles' of fever.

I felt very weak; my depression increased when I realised the risks I should be running if I were forced to spend any length of time in that exposed part of the country, with no help from either human beings or nature itself. My horses were certainly very intelligent animals, of the kind often described as being able to 'do anything but speak'. But speak they could not. They would not have been able to trot off to the nearest village and tell the inhabitants that I was shaking with fever by the roadside.

I summoned up all my resolution and, sitting doubled up in the saddle, with my head bowed over the reins, which I scarcely had the strength to hold, I rode on a little way, abandoning myself to the sure instinct of the animal. To make matters worse rain was falling heavily, drenching my cloak and the manes and hide of the horses. In this state I reached the village of Huari. I should certainly have collapsed after another three or four miles. The residents overwhelmed me with the kindest attentions and supplied me with remedies to cure my sickness. Huari is a brewing centre and a pleasant place to stay at, but it was soon evident that even when ill I could not think of resting. The old trouble about provender for the horses arose. They were given plenty of barley straw, but they refused to touch it.

This difficulty, coupled with the state of my health, led to my being obliged to listen to opinions and advice, proffered with even more persistence than formerly, emphasising the utter folly of continuing my journey. I replied, whenever my shaking and shivering fits allowed me to do so:

"I can't stop now. My mind is made up. I feel that if I turn back it will be as though every horsewoman in my native land had been disgraced. I can't stop——"

I added that the difficulty of feeding the horses was all the more reason for me to ride on as fast as possible to find some place where they could obtain all the fodder they needed.

Eventually I did find such a place, a good distance further on, at a military post where I arrived on the 4th January 1951. I remember the date, because my poor friends then at last obtained everything in the way of food and shelter they had been so longing for. At the garrison town of Challapata, in the quarters of the Ingavi Cavalry, I was enabled to nurse my horses back to complete recovery.

The officers of the regiment treated me with the kindest

consideration and my departure took place amid scenes of genuine enthusiasm. They all signed, in my book, the following inscription: 'Ana Beker: Your ride is an event that deserves the greatest admiration. We cavalrymen consider it a feat of heroism. May you cover the last stage of your journey as fresh and exuberant in spirit as the pampas of your native land. May Principe and Churrito continue to prove your noble and loyal companions.'

In Pazna I changed the horses' 'shoes and stockings'. They certainly needed it. But the farrier, as I was to find later, took his responsibilities rather lightly.

After this I rode right through the tin-mining district of Patino as far as Oruro, its central region, where the richest ores are mined. I was now gradually approaching La Paz. But I still found the journey across this barren tract of country most painful. I got to the point of thinking I should never ride over anything but rocks for the rest of my life. To make matters worse, Principe dropped a shoe and I was therefore obliged to take a short cut, riding downhill whenever possible, through Soledad, Eucaliptus, Lomitas, Biscachani, Calamarca and Viacha. The going was very bad but at last I was able to deposit my weary bones and suffering animals in the railway station at El Alto, a kind of viewpoint or watch-tower overlooking La Paz. My last lap had been one of some forty miles. There was a note of triumph in my sigh of relief, though I was panting a good deal from the altitude, over 13,000 feet. I now got ready to make my entry into the Bolivian capital. I was still riding with difficulty down precipitous slopes as, owing to my horse's having lost a shoe, I did not intend to take any more roundabout routes. I thus shortened the distance to the city by about ten miles.

Chapter VI

FAREWELL TO TWO FAITHFUL FRIENDS

I HAD now reached La Paz where, since I had nowhere else to go, I was put up in the quarters of the Mounted Police. They were kind enough to offer to take every care of my horses. I told them I always fed the animals with my own hand and preferred to do so on this occasion. But they were so insistent that I gave way, only begging them to remember the main point, which was to water the horses before feeding them. I repeated this simple request six or seven times. But the groom did exactly the opposite. Thereupon Principe went down with a most painful colic. I was not informed of his condition for some time. When at last I went to see him everyone in the barracks assembled to watch the poor animal writhing in his agony. I turned pale and could not speak for a moment. Such a violent attack of colic at an altitude of 13,000 feet made me fear the worst. The veterinary surgeon arrived but his attentions only seemed to increase Principe's sufferings. I stormed and raved, seizing and shaking the men in my despair.

"If he dies," I shrieked, "it will be you who have killed him, you murderers!"

Apparently my fury unleashed that of the elements, for a tremendous hailstorm started. As the shed we were in was only an improvised structure and no one wanted to get wet, they all took to their heels at top speed.

"Don't leave him, don't leave him!" I cried. "The hail's not going to kill you!"

But I found myself deserted, alone with Principe. I did everything I could think of to help him. I felt neither the lash of the hail nor the cold, but concentrated on covering the animal with my rainsheet. But in two hours he was dead. At the last moment he had fixed his eyes upon me most intently, uttering a last whinny.

Previously, by putting my arms round him and talking to him as though he were a child, I had managed to make him stand up, though he could not straighten his legs. The last few steps he took were in the direction of his old friend Churrito.

When I saw that he was no longer breathing, that my dear companion over so many paths of incredible difficulty was stiffening in death, I flung my arms round his neck and burst into passionate sobs and weeping. My tears fell incessantly— I cannot remember ever having wept so much in my life. I paid no attention to the passage of time but remained all night by the death bed of my poor friend. I was never again to hear the steady, inspiring music of his hoofs clattering on the rocks nor feel the heave of his flanks as he made a supreme effort to carry me up those practically perpendicular cliffs; never again should I ford rivers on his back as he swam gallantly against the current; never again should I play with him in our moments of leisure, when he used to pull off my hat with his teeth and I would hide behind the rocks, calling his name. It is not easy for those who have never known such a case to realise how fond one can be of an animal. It was even more touching to see how the other horse, Churrito, mourned for his lost companion, as though his own eyes, too, were ready to brim with tears.

As soon as I had dried my tears and mastered my grief I was obliged to consider how to deal with the problem of continuing my journey after suffering this tragic loss.

I decided to compose a telegram directed to Buenos Aires requesting that I might be provided with a remount to enable me to continue on my ride. I mentioned in the telegram that it would be convenient if the horse could be chosen at Salta, this being the Argentine city nearest to La Paz.

I had to stay where I was for a fortnight, by which time I had begun to wonder whether any attention was going to be paid to my request. Then an Argentine police officer, named

Adolfo Nievas, arrived in La Paz, where he quickly make himself at home. Tall, dark and stalwart, he was in every outward respect typical of the glorious old *gauchos* of former times. He had brought a horse with him from Salta, where he was stationed. This animal, a fine type of dappled grey, was called Luchador ('Battler') and was between twelve and thirteen years old. I could not help making a face. The fact was that the grey was very light in colour and I had heard, ever since my childhood, the country superstition that white horses attract misfortune. Moreover, he was an intractable sort of animal of the kind that have to be held down while being shoed.

I had asked in my telegram for a horse from Salta, if possible, as that was the province nearest to Bolivia and consequently there would be less trouble over despatch of the animal. I found that this specimen had been picked out for me by the Governor of the Province, Dr. Costa, an excellent physician but no great connoisseur of horses, least of all of horses of the type I needed.

Nevertheless, I set to work at once to train my new companion for the task in hand, and in particular to get him used to the altitude. The job was a difficult one and required a lot of patience, but I did eventually succeed, and was ready to move off once again.

I had set out from the city and been on the road for two days when my second appalling disaster occurred, near Huarina, on the outskirts of Señor Hanardt's estate. I was riding along the road when a lorry containing two or three Indians, with a white man driving, came towards me. The road at this point ran straight for some miles. Churrito never liked lorries and this one frightened him as usual. As he was jibbing and might have dodged out from our side into the middle of the road, I made clear signs to the driver of the lorry, to indicate that he had better stop or slow down. But the man did nothing of the sort, coming on at the same rate as before. Churrito faced about, presenting his crupper to the crown of the road. He was moving sideways in what is technically called quarter-wheeling. The vehicle struck him head on, the impact flinging him a distance of several yards, to the ditch at the side of the road. The shock of the blow was so violent that the animal's blood spurted out all over me, making me look as if I had also been injured; at first I thought I had been. Then I realised that I had only been stunned for a moment, probably receiving internal bruises, the animal having fallen on top of me. The mutilated carcass of the poor beast lay a few paces from me. I jumped up in a frenzy of grief and rage, then flung myself, in a tempest of weeping, on the dead horse. The driver of the lorry had only slowed down for a moment. Then he had accelerated on at a higher speed than ever.

Some Indians had collected round me and were shouting: "Run, Missie, run! That lorry man will have to pay for this!"

At the same moment Churrito whinnied, cast a despairing glance at me and breathed his last. I kissed his muzzle, dried my tears, mounted Luchador and set off at full gallop after the lorry, after calling to the men in the road:

"Keep off those wheel-tracks!"

I meant to prove that the vehicle had driven on to my side of the road.

My first attempts to report this crime met with a blank wall of indifference. I wanted to send a telegram. But they wouldn't tell me to whom it should be addressed. At the Transport Office the clerks shrugged their shoulders. None of them could trace the number of the lorry. It seemed as though they were all in league together. At last I complained to the Governor. A little later the lorry driver was arrested, though they could have laid hands on him long before. The tedious processes of the law dragged on in La Paz. Once more I was obliged to remain in the city, as if it were not enough that the loss of Churrito had almost broken my heart.

Litigation with the driver went on and on. Interviews with lawyers and offers to settle the matter out of court succeeded one another. Then I had a row with the Director of Transport, who wanted to put a summary end to the whole business. He shouted and I shouted. He thumped the table with his fist and I thumped it with my whip. Luckily he proved to be a decent fellow after all and we soon patched up our quarrel. He did all he could for me and when I left La Paz he sent a motorised column to see me out of the city.

As for the driver who had caused the accident, on being reprimanded for his carelessness he calmly answered:

"I saw them coming along, but thought it was an Indian with the horses."

Señor Tesler Reyes, a member of the Bolivian Parliament, called on the Argentine consul and offered to present me with a mare to replace Churrito. She was a fourteen-year-old chestnut. This gift and the reimbursement of my hospital expenses compensated me to some extent for my troubles. I did not feel, however, that a mare was exactly what I wanted for so gruelling a ride. Mares are a nuisance in some ways, with their seasons of heat and other somewhat inconvenient habits. Altogether, what with one misfortune and another, the lawsuit and various other delays and adversities, I was held up at La Paz for one month and twenty-five days.

I had time to explore this picturesque and up-to-date city at my leisure. It had been founded in 1548 and had long been a base and source of supply for the mining communities nearer the coast, as well as exporting the coca-leaf grown in the Yunga district, by chewing which the Indian peasant secures his illusory artificial paradise. The city contains buildings surviving from the colonial period, such as the church of San Francisco with its façade and interior features of granite, carved by native stone-masons, and other architectural treasures like the Villaverde ancestral residence, with its coat of arms and motto in Spanish, 'My sword may be shattered but my faith will not be found wanting'. These buildings, though they date from the colonial period, bear distinct traces of the native style, with its reminders of the ancient civilisation of the country. On the other hand the newest parts of the city are thoroughly up to date. They include the modern El Prado Avenue and that named after General Camacho, in the centre of the business quarter, a modern arterial road flanked by cement-built skyscrapers. Modern also are the Law Courts and such striking monuments as the statue of Marshal Sucre. Yet care is taken, too, to preserve the most typical and charming of the old streets that recall colonial days, with their narrow, cobbled pavements and flights of stone steps.

In spite of all that happened at La Paz my recollections of the city are on the whole agreeable ones. I was given a most ceremonious send-off, with a motorised escort and shrill blasts on the town's sirens. Señor Burgos, President of the Argentine Club, was present at the celebrations and I was entreated to think kindly of Bolivia in spite of the unlucky chance by which I had lost two horses there.

Shortly after leaving the city I found myself in a district of many lakes and rivers, impassable to cars, though horses, with considerable difficulty, could get through.

I rode on with my horse and my mare, passed Pucarini and Huasina, and eventually reached Tiquino and Lake Titicaca. I had already ridden past other great lakes such as that of Poopo in the south of the country. But on this occasion I was struck with amazement and admiration at the sight of those crystalline waters, smooth and limpid as a vast emerald. Unlike rivers and ordinary lakes their lucid depths reflected nothing but the sky and its clouds, so that the surface presented a uniform aspect of motionless tranquillity. It seems that Lake Titicaca is fed by a continuous current that then flows out of it into the river Desaguadero, so that the water is always fresh. The story is told that in the eighteenth century, when the level of the lake sank, the heads of certain statues erected in the time of the old civilisation appeared above the surface. The owners of the adjoining land carried the statues off to adorn their estates, whereupon a series of disasters occurred and the superstitious owners dropped the statues back into the lake. Some say that the legendary city of Chiopata, so often mentioned by archaeologists and explorers, lies buried beneath the waters.

One feels inclined to accept almost any plausible tale when confronted with the mysterious and magical beauty of this vast necklace of water lying beneath the ramparts of the mountains, inaccessible, apparently, to mankind.

For this reason I was not so much surprised as I might logically have been by the episode I am about to relate. I was riding along one of the lakeside paths when I became aware that someone, no doubt an Indian, was following me at a certain distance, scrambling over the rocks. After a time I reined in the horses to wait for him. He called out to me and approached with the evident intention of speaking to me. His face was so deeply tanned and furrowed with so many wrinkles that he might have been a centenarian. He may have been eighty years old; it was impossible to say. His only companion was a black llama with white ears, its back loaded with small saddle-bags. He asked me, in obscure but intelligible Spanish, a number of searching questions. What was I doing, why was I doing it and how did I manage to do it, in such a desolate place, so far, to judge from my appearance and dress, from everything that was familiar to me? I replied as politely and tactfully as I could to this respectable old fellow, who continued to stare at me in amazement.

As soon as his curiosity was satisfied he informed me that he would like to tell me something more important than anything I had ever heard in my life. As I did not feel in the least afraid of him I sat down beside him to listen to his secret. He declared that at the bottom of the lake, at a spot which he knew perfectly well, coins of an incalculable value were to be found, together with a great number of statues and other objects, made of solid gold and of silver, which had belonged to ancient kings who had ruled thousands of years ago. It was true that all this treasure at present lay deep under water. But he had invented, he said, a system of wooden stakes and ropes of vicuna wool by means of which many of the objects in question could be hauled to the surface.

I began to think he was merely spinning me a yarn. But to make sure I interrupted him by saying:

"You and I would never be able to lift all that up from the bottom of the lake by ourselves."

He answered emphatically that he knew exactly where best to operate and that two people like ourselves could easily do it by means of his system. He added that he considered no one to be so suitable a person to transport such hidden treasure as a woman with two powerful horses who was riding all over the world. My job would be to load up these valuable objects and take them to a place where they could be converted into plenty of money. I had heard that serious excavators working on the shores of the lake had unearthed all sorts of articles, such as jewels, wine-jars and carvings that proved the existence of a high standard of artistic creation thousands of years ago. And although I continued to be extremely sceptical about the old Indian's fantastic talk, the majestic environment of that unpeopled solitude, the poetic suggestion of the rose-and-violet-coloured mountains and the enchanting beauty of the lake all predisposed me to imagine there might be some truth in his mysterious tale.

It would give me no trouble to follow him to the place he had spoken of. It would only be one more stage, anyhow, on my long road, so I consented to accompany him to the scene of operations. This decision necessitated a delay of some hours in order to wait for nightfall, when, in fact, brilliant moonlight illuminated the mountains and was reflected from the rocks and the lake, turning all to a mass of quicksilver that seemed to come from another world. We were about to commence our task when the Indian exclaimed, with every sign of terror, that he had just seen the shadow of one of the evil spirits of the lake, which was particularly and cruelly hostile to the seekers of hidden treasure, and that accordingly there could be no question of proceeding with our plan for another week.

As may be imagined, I had no intention of waiting for even one more night, let alone seven, and I thought it best to tell him so.

"I'm on my way to Peru now," I told him. "But within a week I shall be back with the horses and we can then raise all the treasure we can get at."

"Couldn't you bring an additional pair of horses?" he asked. "There may be a good deal to lift, you know."

His idea was, roughly, that we should divide into two parts the enormous sum which we should receive in exchange for the articles I was to take to the countries where very rich and fair-complexioned people lived. He would then spend his share on the purchase of land in some fertile valley and end his days in opulent luxury.

I did not tell him that such a procedure would be impossible, for that would have been useless. Nor did I even try to find out whether he had been lying to me. My business was to continue my journey. I hurried on, crossing the lake of Titicaca at its narrowest part in a big sailing vessel aboard which I was allowed to embark the horses. At this point the crossing can be made very quickly, whereas the wider sections need a whole night in a ferryboat for the passage. I had made up my mind already that throughout the ride my horses were only to be subjected to the indispensable minimum of transport by water or any other means, otherwise I considered my whole project would lose its unique character and I should be guilty of a sort of fraud.

CHAPTER VII

CONDORS OVER CUZCO

W E soon reached the further bank of Lake Titicaca and I then had to choose between proceeding along easy roads which would lead me a long way round, or following the tortuous Indian tracks across the mountains. I decided to take the latter course. But those Indian tracks scarcely deserved the name and were barely suitable for human beings, much less for the weight of horses. And they continually staggered and often fell to their knees as if they had lost heart altogether. Some ten miles from Titicaca the mare missed her footing on a very steep slope and went reeling and sliding downhill, with me on her back, till a few good-sized rocks brought us to a standstill. I was bruised all over and feared that the mare might have done herself a serious injury. Meanwhile Luchador had taken fright and got into a position which might well have ended in a similarly dangerous tumble. The mare, whose name was Pobre India, got to her feet luckily without much trouble and I then had to face the task of calming the two animals while trying to keep my balance on the slope; this operation took over an hour. At last I succeeded in mounting Pobre India. I could not change to Luchador because the mare was a bad follower, and no good as a pack-horse.

After this troublesome passage, I entered Copacabana, where the inhabitants gave me a kind reception. The chief of the frontier police, Captain Ciro Montaño, wrote in my travel diary: 'I wish the valiant Argentine horsewoman, Ana Beker, every sort of good fortune in her unparalleled feat of endurance and earnestly hope she may acquire for her country, and all devotees of sport in this continent the laurels gained by her athletic prowess, the first of its kind ever to be re-corded. Good luck and may God be with her.'

At the Kasani frontier post, where Bolivian territory ends, I saw, for the last time during my journey, the red, yellow and green flag of Bolivia. It was the 14th March, 1951. Then I set foot in Peru. Customs formalities hardly existed, for both Peruvians and Bolivians consider an Argentine citizen to be practically a compatriot.

I was to leave Bolivia with some sad memories, for in that country where the landscapes had made so deep an impression on me, I had left my two dear companions; Principe and Churrito lay buried in the Bolivian earth. I went my way without them, but I should never forget them nor the hard yet not unrewarding roads we had travelled together.

In the first Peruvian town I came to the authorities decorated my diary with ribbons of the national colours, red and white.

My first contacts with the aboriginal natives of that beautiful country, where I was later to find so much to admire, proved far from agreeable. It just happened that to begin with I came across nothing but the most poverty-stricken little hamlets, where I was even obliged to witness a scene in which certain of the inhabitants picked lice off the bodies of others and subsequently ate the insects. They spent their primitive existence in huts of wood and straw. But they possessed a rude kind of organisation, for in every village and district a headman ruled, to whom every traveller of an unusual sort, like myself, who might arrive at any hour of the day or night, had to report.

One reason why I have stated that my first contacts with these people were far from agreeable is that when on one occasion I let my horses graze at the side of the road an Indian woman immediately rushed up to them, making signs to me that the animals could not be allowed to eat there. She told me the same thing in Kechuan, the Peruvian Indian dialect, and repeated it in bad Spanish. As may be imagined, I ignored her protests. She then, in a fearful rage, uttering exclamations which I suppose were insulting, engaged in a rather comic performance. With all the haste she could muster she began tearing the grass out of the mouths of the horses. But the animals, hungry as they always were on such occasions, ate so fast that her interference did not succeed in depriving them of their meal. I could not help laughing as I watched her. The woman's fury rose to a climax. She seized a stick and started beating the animals. Luchador, the grey, let fly twice with his heels and only just missed the obstinate creature's head. Thereupon, evidently supposing that I would be an easier mark, she advanced upon me, flourishing her cudgel. I picked up and raised my whip. As it was necessary to give her a fright and send her packing I told her that she would regret it if she dared to attack me. She instantly bent down to snatch up a stone and the next moment it went whistling past my eyes. She followed it up with a further charge, waving her stick.

I shouted at her in my best patois: "If you want to fight, come on. You can taste my whip and a bullet from my revolver, too, if you like!"

The woman's attitude changed in a flash. She spun round and tore off as fast as her legs would carry her till she was out of sight.

I had been quietly watching the grazing horses for some time when I heard some deafening yells; some fifty people, men, women and children, were running up the road towards me, screaming at the tops of their voices. Next moment a shower of stones rained down on the animals and myself. One of these missiles caught me such a hard blow on the knee that I could not bend it for quite a while. Two pretty big stones hit the mare's head and brought her to her knees, though she stood up again directly afterwards. There was obviously no time to lose; I drew my revolver, sprang on to Luchador, and galloped bareback full tilt at the Indians firing two shots in the air as I did so. This had the effect I had anticipated. The whole crowd scattered, each one running as if the devil were after him.

This incident did not make me bear the Indians any grudge, for later on, as I shall relate, I received many benefits from them. I was always delighted when I met, as I rode along, one of those little Indian boys, with his round, shining face, resembling a copper coin, his circular hat and his ragged little cloak, leading by a halter a *paco*, one of those superbly graceful animals belonging to the llama family and so typical of Peru. When their wool is fully grown it covers them all over, falls over their eyes and nearly sweeps the ground, as if they were dressed in a large blanket. They are a different breed from the *alpaca* and *vicuña* of Peru.

My arrival in Cuzco, or rather my short stay in that city, was unforgettable. I shall always remember this city of the Incas, with the gigantic snowy peaks of Salkantay and Ausangati dominating the most impressive of all horizons.

I took the opportunity to admire, among other archaeological treasures, the imposing ruins of the buildings of the Inca period. One has always heard a great deal about them, but it is only when one sees them with one's own eyes that one is overcome by the magnitude of their achievement. As I drew near the remains of the Inca city of Machupichu I saw that it lay penned between the peaks of the Andes in the wildest possible surroundings, near the clouds caught in the snare of the mountain tops, as though we had left all other earthly things far below us.

The name of the city means 'Ancient Summit' and few places in America or in the whole world can compare with it for the grandeur of its situation in the Urubamba gorge. It is astonishing to think that buildings could have been constructed at so tremendous a height. Obviously the native workmen had to begin by cutting vast stairways of thousands of steps in the living rock, as well as the whole system of stairs, terraces and platforms which apparently served as means of communication between the temples, houses, palaces and tombs. The monument called the Torreón, or great tower, standing on a huge soaring rock of formidable dimensions, impressed me more deeply than anything else among the ruins.

I also visited the ruins on the banks of the Vilcanota, at Pisac and Tampumachay; the latter are said to be the remains of the residence where the Inca himself spent his leisure.

The whole neighbourhood might be called the Kingdom of the Rocks. It is the living rock which give it so impressive a character of eternal permanence. The towers, the observatories and the mighty buttresses of every stronghold are built of rock, unbroken slabs nearly forty feet high. There are serried ranks of rocks, rocks set on end and gigantic hewn rocks such as are found in the ruins of Ollantaytambo and all the walls built in the Inca period, vast assemblages of geometrically shaped and polished stones that bear mute witness to the immense labour that must have been required and the impregnability of the result.

I gazed for long at the twelve-cornered stone in the street called Hatunrumioc at Cuzco, which is supposed to be one of the oldest and strangest monuments of ancient Peru; it is certainly a comprehensive example of the mysterious art of the Inca people, being embedded in a still existent house, once the Hatunrumioc Palace. I also explored the amphitheatre, with its walls resembling a series of thrones, among the ruins of Kenko.

Precious specimens of colonial architecture can also be found in Cuzco; not for nothing is the city called the archaeological capital of South America. I am no archaeologist, nor am I writing a book on ancient architecture, but it was long before the vision faded from my memory of such colonial masterpieces as the cathedral and the Convent of Mercy.

Stirred to wonder and admiration as I was by such impressions, it was the Andean landscape itself, nature's own wild, free and inimitable architecture, that most captivated my mind. Some soaring crag, leaping to the very sky from its escorting squadrons of rocks of a thousand varied shapes, took a deeper hold upon my imagination than any of the works of man.

After leaving Cuzco I was riding through open country when I caught sight of a large body of horsemen. As they drew nearer I noticed that many of them were well mounted and rode in expert fashi   with no resemblance at all to the Indian style. There were, indeed, some aboriginals among them. But they looked quite different from those with whom I was familiar.

At first I felt rather uneasy, thinking they might have some intention of attacking or robbing me. But when they came within earshot I could hear them cheering me enthusiastically. They welcomed me with the greatest kindness.

They all escorted me to a big country house in the neighbourhood, the property of Señor Abel Pacheco. It was this courteous and amiable gentleman who, after he had taken leave of me himself in the city, had sent out his servants and friends to bring me to his estate. On arrival there I was entertained, with a hospitality I shall never forget, by Señora Elena Gonzalez, a friend of the owner. The time I spent on this estate was one of the most enjoyable stages of my journey. It was a long time since I had seen country-bred horsemen with real skill in riding, though here they did not achieve quite the same high standard of devotion, versatility and mastery of equitation as the gauchos of my own native land.

The contrast with Argentina became still more marked when, shortly afterwards, I found myself in the most precipitous region of the Andes, where there were no roads and the peaks and gorges of the landscape presented a continuous panorama of terrifying grandeur.

It was soon after this that I was confronted by an impressive and alarming spectacle that will never fade from my memory. It happened while I was sitting on the edge of an extremely narrow and winding path beside a precipice and was deep in contemplation of the mighty buttresses and tremendous cliffs of the mountains, in all their awe-inspiring splendour. The horses stood a few yards away, also taking great care with their movements, for in this sort of country one must never forget that one false step might send one hurtling into the abyss. Luchador had gone slightly further off in search of jujube-trees, which grew at rare intervals among the rocks.

I had already watched on several occasions the majestic flight of the condors, as they passed between the crags or alighted on them. When one of these birds perched on some towering crest and stood outlined against the dazzling sky in an attitude of intent vigilance, one felt as though in the presence of a true king of the Andes.

Suddenly I saw a condor of great size sweep by, flying very fast, like a diving aircraft. It almost touched Luchador. The first condor was followed by another. Then came three or four more. They flew round in a wide arc and then returned to pass the horse again. The animal showed distinct signs of uneasiness. One of the great birds, as it shot past, dealt the horse a violent blow with its wing. The next followed suit. Then, to my own terror and amid the panic-stricken plunging of Luchador, the huge birds started striking at the animal right and left, with their enormous wings. After a moment I realised what they meant to do. They were trying to make the horse lose its footing on the path and roll down the precipice into the chasm below.

I reached Luchador just in time to seize his bridle and prevent his blindly stumbling movements from sending him over the edge.

When the condors saw me come to the rescue they rose slightly higher in the air than they had before, but only to return to the charge. They seemed furiously determined to achieve their purpose. A regular struggle ensued, for the horse became unmanageable at times in his terror. I kept yelling at the big birds and waving my arms like a windmill to frighten them away. At last they flew off to a short distance. I then tethered the horse to a heavy rock and went back to where I had left my baggage. I fired three or four shots from my revolver. The reports sent the great birds far enough away for me to lead the horses to a less exposed and precarious spot.

This episode was one of the most terrifying of my whole ride. The ferocious birds stayed in the neighbourhood for some time before they finally vanished, disappointed of their prey.

I had not realized that condors would attack large animals in such a way but I heard later that they often do adopt these tactics in the case of donkeys, mules or horses of no great size which have been left to themselves due to sickness or old age. The birds are easily able to make them lose their footing in steep places and fall over the precipices by attacking them in the manner described. When the animals have been killed by the fall condors arrive from all directions to feed on the carcases till they have picked the bones clean. I myself saw on a steep slope, near Abancay, a lean old mule in poor condition, which had no doubt strayed from a drove on the march, attacked by condors in this way. They knocked the animal down, and as it rolled downhill struck it with their wings. I entered the ravine into which the animal had fallen and saw the condors furiously tearing and pecking at it. Dozens of vultures suddenly appeared from heaven knows where, for I never saw them come, and circled in the air above the carrion. When the condors had satisfied their hunger the vultures replaced them; between them they left very little of the hapless mule.

The way out of Abancay led down a series of enormous precipices that seriously endangered the lives of my horses. We had reached the central region of the mountains. Tremendous peaks shut in the horizon on all sides. It was impossible to ride. I went forward on foot, leading the horses. They were thus liable to slip and fall on top of me, and before long this happened. The mare sent me flying and when I tried to rise I felt severe pains in one leg. I thought I had broken it and that I would have to lie up for heaven knew how long. Luckily, however, I managed to go on walking and as the warmth returned to my limbs I found that I need not have worried. The road from Abancay to San Gabriel and from San Gabriel to La Hacienda Pampatama, thirty-two miles further on, and thence to Chalhuanca, another thirty-four miles, is called the Promesa. I found it one of the most difficult stages of my journey, for it was known as the 'lorry smasher'. It had been built as a motor-road but designed in so reckless a fashion that accident statistics were mounting day by day.

Near Pampamarca I spent the night in an Indian village 13,000 feet above sea-level. The headman mobilised his subjects in force to collect food and help my horses to recover their strength. I was agreeably surprised by the solicitude he showed and the praise he lavished on the two animals. But I soon found out the reason. The headman was very keen for me to barter one of my horses, the pack-animal, for four or five of his llamas. He affirmed that if I divided up my baggage among the llamas and rode my own gallant mare I could cross the mountains without difficulty. I did my best to convince him that his llamas would be no use to me in the extremely variegated types of country that I should have to traverse and equally that the horse would be just as little use to him among the mountain passes and trackless wildernesses of the Andes. At last I found myself obliged to refuse his request point-blank, and prove to him that my horse would only give him trouble. I pretended to try to get hold of Luchador's hoof as though to shoe it, so that the headman could see for himself the kicks and bites in all directions that this procedure caused. I added that in order to shoe the horse it would be necessary for several men to throw him down and hold him by force. Further, as I had pretty good control over Luchador, I signed to him to snatch off the chief's cloak, which he did by seizing it in his teeth. After this, nothing more was said about the proposed exchange. I continued my journey for another long stretch, my destination being Puquio, 190 miles from Abancay.

Between the Promesa road and Puquio I had to cross an unbroken desert plateau, the worst sort of country of all as there was no grazing for the horses. The whole of this continuous table-land lies at more than 13,000 feet above sea-level. At any cost I had to find something for my companions to eat, and I took every opportunity of leaving the mountain track in search of something for them to bite on, as the inhabitants of the villages we came across often had nothing to offer.

I could see that the summits and the highest ranges of the mountains were covered with snow. Soon it began to lie thickly over the ground we were traversing. Snow fell for the whole of one day and was still falling as night came on. Before long drifts began to block the road. We could not find the smallest village and according to my map there was no settlement of any size anywhere near. The desolate Andean night closed down upon us. It seemed as though mankind had died out. The horses, I thought, might well freeze to death. At last I discovered, almost by chance, a small aperture, a sort of cave, among the rocks, and sat down in it after covering the animals with my blankets.

That night was another bad one. I was terribly frightened and imagined that the snow was going to bury all three of us and prove our winding-sheet. I realised that there had been no exaggeration in the constant warnings I had been given of the dangers of this cruel region.

On this occasion I could not even master my fears when, in the grey, pallid light of dawn, I managed, after shaky efforts with my swollen fingers, to saddle up and mount, in defiance of the pains that afflicted my limbs as the frost gripped them. Cold, one of the great enemies of travellers in the open air, fastened its clutches upon me. It is true that, taking my journey as a whole, I should be bound to record many more days of distress spent in torrid heat beneath an implacable sun rather than in the grip of intense cold. But I suffered none the less for that reason from the days of cold.

The desert landscape grew steadily more deserted. I did however come across a few small farms and villages where the aboriginal occupants offered me the brandy known as *Pisco*, from the Peruvian seaport of that name, to warm me, recommending me earnestly not to despise it. If I did not drink it, they all told me, the cold would end by freezing up my bones and blood for ever. They were not far wrong, as a matter of fact. I often found great draughts of that burning liquor an excellent tonic.

At Negro Mayo, 14,000 feet above sea-level, the temperature dropped till it became unbearable. My hands froze to the reins. I lost all sensation in my feet and the skin of my whole face hardened and cracked. The bristles on the horses' hides were standing up. It was most dangerous to halt them in the open at that temperature. There was no question of lighting a fire to warm us, as wood did not exist. I could find no branches anywhere within reach.

After a few days of this sort of thing we began to go down-hill and the cold grew less intense. I discovered to my relief that neither I myself nor the horses had caught pneumonia or suffered any other serious injury.

The landscape continued bleak and deserted; for miles at a stretch it seemed practically uninhabited, and I was obliged to press on as fast as possible to avoid having to spend too many nights in places so utterly destitute of comfort. From seven in the morning until well after nightfall I rode without stopping, trotting all the time as if I were being pursued. I was in fact being pursued by hunger, which also threatened my two animals. It is not easy for others to imagine the extent to which food and nourishment for the horses become an obsession. I dreamed of heaped-up bundles of fodder, of vast plains of lucerne and great bags of barley.

A motorist, for instance, who has to drive thousands and thousands of miles may often find himself faced with long stretches where there are no filling stations. In my case the tank had to be filled every twenty-four hours without fail and I could think of nothing else. I would not wish my worst enemy to suffer what I felt when I had to watch my poor beasts starving. I saw them staggering in their exhaustion and longing to drop to the ground with no more strength to go on carrying me and my baggage on their backs. I have seen them nibbling in desperation at the bark of a tree-trunk and seizing between their teeth anything green or straw-coloured that protruded between the rocks. I have seen them eat their own dung, glancing at me before doing so as if they were ashamed of being driven to such an extremity. It was an indescribable look, half apology and half despair. As a rule I used the whip to stop them from resorting to any such expedient. But sometimes I had to let them have their will.

During our long wanderings the animals had to eat the most extraordinary things, including roots, maize-leaves, carob beans and bananas, as their only food for days.

CHAPTER VIII

PERUVIAN MAGIC

DURING my journey through that desolate stretch of country I met a band of people who had come to visit its deserted valleys. They were Peruvians, though not of the Indian race, and hunters of the *vicuña*. The wool of this animal is very useful and profitable; many garments are made of it, especially the cloaks woven by the skilful craftsmen of the country, in bright and tasteful combinations of colours.

At this period strict laws forbade the hunting of the *vicuña* in this part of Peru. Nevertheless, certain bold hunters took the risk, all the more eagerly on account of the high value set on game shot in defiance of these laws; they employed highly trained hounds, which rounded up the *vicuñas* and drove them in the direction of the guns.

My presence in those parts greatly surprised these gentry. As they were the sort of people who do not care for any witnesses of their operations, they took up a highly suspicious attitude when they first saw me and their examination of my appearance did not do much to allay their misgivings. The fact that I was a woman threw them into still greater perplexity.

They surrounded me with their rifles well in evidence and demanded whether I had any connection with the Government, the Civil Guard or official authority of any kind.

I made the mistake of thinking it might be as well to make some reference to my credentials on this occasion.

"Yes," I said. "The Government is, in a sense, aware of and authorises my——"

I meant that the Argentine Government knew about my ride, but my questioners were far from delighted with my reply.

"Oh, so they're employing young ladies in trousers with horses to carry out inspections of the mountains nowadays, are they?"

"I'm not doing any inspecting."

One of the hunters gave the show away—"There's nothing to inspect, anyhow. You can't prove that we've killed a single head of game."

"Well, I did hear a few shots, you know."

The most resolute of the hunters levelled his rifle at me. "Oh, did you? Well, you're going to swear to us, here and now, that you didn't hear or see anything. Otherwise I'll pump you full of lead. Understand?"

He thrust the muzzle of his shotgun against my breast.

"I'm not interested," I protested, "in anything you're doing or in anything I may have seen or heard. I'm from Argentina."

The man lowered his weapon.

"You mentioned the Government——"

"I meant the Argentine Government."

"Well, that's different. But what on earth——"

I explained the situation, as I had done so many hundreds of times that it sounded like a gramophone record, telling them about my plans and the nature of the journey I was undertaking. I don't think they had much idea what I was talking about but I seemed to convince them, in the end, that they had nothing to fear from me. They proceeded to compliment me on my unusual method of arriving in the country and even invited me to fire, if I liked, at one of the vicuñas rounded up by the hounds, if I should catch sight of one. I did take the opportunity of discharging a gun, which one of them handed me, at a vicuña. But I deliberately missed the target, so as not to be guilty of any infraction of the law.

When I remounted to take leave of the hunters, they insisted on my telling them plainly whether I intended to make any mention of their activities to any official I might happen to meet. I answered that I would delay doing so as long as possible. Then, as I put spurs to my horse and trotted off, I called back to them:

"If they don't ask me I shan't say anything; but if they do I shall have to answer!"

One of the hunters, in a rage, threw up his gun to his shoulder. But the man next him prevented him from firing, if that had been his intention, and I rode off without turning round again.

For some days after this incident I met no one but the inhabitants of Indian villages, and throughout the Peruvian stage of my journey I had plenty of opportunities to talk with the aboriginal occupants of the country. Racially, they are the survivors of the magnificent Inca civilisation and its intermixture with the subject Andean population. Since the time when Manco Capao, whose father was the Sun, and his wife and sister Mama Oclo, founded their empire in this part of the world, many centuries have passed. I don't know the exact number, but they are said to have been very many. They have not been numerous enough to extinguish altogether in these people the special characteristics of their race. Some of the village headmen feel themselves to be as important in their sphere as any of the ancient leaders of their nation or even as Pachacutec, Tupa-Yupanqui or Huayna-Capac, themselves, the most powerful and famous of the Incas.

For my own part, when I remember my dealings with the present-day Indians, a placid, poverty-stricken and far from powerful race, I can recall that they afforded me every assistance in the course of my journey, as well as my horses. I also found useful the medical remedies which they offered me from their abundant store of such things. These remedies might well be called primitive or rustic. But in many cases they proved strangely effective. I often saw the Indians apply such remedies as powdered and greased bitumen for closing ulcers, *millu* earth, or natural iron sulphate, for suppurating pustules and *tacu* bark for relieving dysentery. They also used *copaquira*, a bluish, transparent stone, to disinfect wounds, and *coravari*, a green stone in powdered form, for insect bites and the same concoction in a much diluted form to clear the vision and prevent excessive watering of the eyes. I myself was occasionally obliged to make use of the remedies offered me by the Indians. I remember, for instance, suffering from a painful inflammation of the throat which disappeared when I gargled with a liquid prepared from the leaves of the plant called *quina* (cinchona) or *payco*. The medicine-man made me sit on the ground in front of him and pour the liquid into my mouth under his intent gaze.

I have never been really prejudiced against such domestic or traditional cures as I was brought up in the country and often saw how effective such cures were, as much in the case of human beings as in that of animals.

I had the chance to examine closely a large number of different medicaments of this kind, as for nearly two whole days I had the company of a voluntary guide and fellow-traveller in the shape of a typical example of the wandering physician of that part of the country. These men undertake on foot, or occasionally on a mule, journeys of immense length and even through foreign countries. I saw no reason why I should not accept this man's services, as I always had need of guides. The appearance, moreover, of this nomad practitioner of the Andes struck me as remarkably respectable and even kindly. He did not look more than forty, though an infinite number of wrinkles furrowed his face and hands, which had the appearance of dried mud; all sorts of medals, crucifixes and amulets hung round his neck.

When we pulled up to water and rest the horses, he showed me innumerable samples of his herbal remedies. They included *carbincho* for intestinal trouble, *silla* for getting rid of bile, *itapalo* for difficulty in passing urine, *aratuk* for a stitch in the side, *payapulla* for ulcers and tumours, *mangapaqui* for rheumatism and a host of others. Nor did his simple cures consist only of vegetable matter. I remember that there was an insect with black and red spots which, when ground to powder, cured ulcers. There were also other repulsive little creatures which had a diuretic or soothing effect and further properties to which there seemed no end, not to mention various kinds of shagreen, *quincho* grease and so on.

I was a bit disconcerted when I heard the medicine-man say that soup made from the flesh of a young kite could restore the mentally afflicted to the use of their faculties, that a cut from the wing of a condor placed upon the stomach of a pregnant woman could facilitate delivery and that the powdered flesh of the humming-bird cured epilepsy.

In general, I only listened out of curiosity to my companion's account of his remedies and the verbal spells and formulae of witchcraft he used, which made up a positive encyclopaedia. I remained anxious about the risk of catching malaria, against which I had been warned over and over again. I had even been given a detailed description of the zones on my route or near it which were chiefly affected by this disease in Peru. I was well aware, in common with everyone else, of the importance of quinine in this connection. But my medicine-man companion told me that still more effective remedies were the viscous juice of the prickly pear and also that of a cactus he named, as well as that of other plants he would be able to give me, which were all essentially anti-malarial.

I watched my voluntary companion go into action in a small village of natives' huts. He first asked some boys who were in charge of a flock of llamas if there were any sick people in the place. It seemed that the putting of this question was his usual procedure. The boys told him of a family where there was a woman lying seriously ill. He went straight to the house and, without offering his services, made his presence obvious. He was waiting for them to call him in, which they eventually did. As I had grown accustomed to regarding the medicine-man as one far above the sordid temptations of this world I was astonished to see how patiently, yet firmly, without yielding an inch of ground, he discussed the question of his remuneration in kind. He asked the patient a number of questions in the ancient Peruvian language, which I did not understand. Then he dropped a few coca-leaves on her breast and stomach. When the leaves fell off on to the ground he noted exactly where they fell. Next, he left the hut, stood for some time gazing fixedly at the sky and then, after uttering a few words which not even the Indians present understood, he told the members of the sick woman's family that she was bewitched and that her malady came from a small animal which he said he could find for them. He walked a little way out of the village, moved round in circles for a while and finally pointed out a place at which he advised them to dig. They soon unearthed a toad, which had been securely tied up, so that it could not move. It seemed to be dead. But when the medicine-man untied it the animal, after some considerable time, began to move and finally crawled away. The Indians all gave a shout of triumph, convinced that the sick woman had been released from the spell now that the toad had been released. They gave the medicine-man more than he had asked in payment for his services and most of the villagers came a good part of the way with us on our departure, showing every sign of gratitude.

I don't propose to give myself a headache wondering how my companion managed to perform this mysterious conjuring trick. Had he himself buried the toad before joining me on my way? It was queer that the animal had contrived to survive. Or had he arranged with someone else to have it buried in that fashion? In any case, whether such methods succeed only by working on the superstitions of the aboriginals or whether there may be some sense in them after all, it cannot be denied that occasionally these primitive medicine-men achieve cures that no one else can manage. At all events, the abrupt way in which this wandering physician subsequently vanished had something very like witchcraft about it. Night surprised us in a place where we could find a little shelter until daylight. We lay down, wrapping ourselves in our blankets. Before going to sleep my companion gave me a leaf of the aloe plant, a few pine-twigs and a fragment of the foot of some bird or other. He advised me either to keep these things always on my person or else bury them in some place which I should never forget. If I did the former and found myself in serious danger, it would be enough for me to touch the pouch containing these objects. I should then escape whatever peril it might be. In the second case all I would have to do would be to concentrate on remembering the place where I had buried the pouch.

I was dozing rather than sleeping as I lay some twenty or thirty yards away from the man, close to my horses. As soon as dawn broke I opened my eyes to look for the medicine-man but he had disappeared. I couldn't see a single trace of him and I never saw or heard of him again.

As I did not wish to disregard his instructions entirely I buried the pouch he had given me. It really seemed as though my sorcerer had vanished into thin air. I then continued my journey to Nasca and thence to Pisco. From that town I followed the direct coast road northwards for a considerable distance.

During this part of the ride I obtained several more signatures for my record-book, ranging from those of leading members of the aboriginal communities to those of officers of the Civil Guard, chairmen of local Councils and Justices of the Peace.

The road ran steadily downhill till it came in sight of the great city of Lima, a thirsty spot, but full of flowers. I arrived there on the 8th May 1951.

CHAPTER IX

SUNSTROKE, HUNGER AND AN EARTHQUAKE

I FOUND Lima to be an oasis where I rested and found entertainment everywhere. I shall confine myself to mentioning the hospitality I received from the Pinerolo and Peru Racing Clubs and from the Jockey Club. A group of representatives of the Pinerolo rode out to meet me at Mount Limatambu; they formed a splendid body of horsemen. Saluting me from the saddle, they overwhelmed me with compliments and congratulations; I shall always remember them. These friendly and distinguished horse-lovers spared no efforts to make my stay in the city a pleasant one. Luchador, the horse so kindly sent me from Argentina, was not really proving up to my requirements and the mare was no use as a pack-horse, I had to ride her instead of the other, which rather added to my difficulties in the stages between La Paz and Lima.

I allowed these facts to become known in riding circles at Lima and was lucky enough to find a sympathetic hearing among the Argentine colony in the city. They enlisted the aid of the Argentine ambassador, General Vago, and of his Secretary for Labour, Bengacio di Pascuale, with a view to helping me out of my difficulties.

The Minister for War, General Zanon Noriega, with the consent of President Odria, gave orders for a horse to be presented to me.

The Minister extended his good offices towards myself and Argentina, since at least from a sporting point of view I represented my country, to the point of arranging that the animal should be selected from those at the San Martin military headquarters. When the order was transmitted to the officers of the station they contrived to spirit their best mounts away before I came to look them over. It was natural enough, of course, for them to try to avoid being deprived of one of their favourites. When I arrived I could not see one that really suited me; I guessed what they had been up to.

"Gentlemen," I told them, laughing, "I really can't believe that none of the horses at a headquarters of the Peruvian Army come above the average."

"Well, of course, you're used to the Argentine breed," said one.

"We hear that some Argentine horses are equal to any in the world," went on another.

I noticed a brief and highly significant smile, for an instant, on the face of one of the subalterns.

"Look here," I said. "I'm rather pressed for time to-day and it would take me quite a few hours to make a choice. I'll come back in four or five days, when I shall have more leisure."

But instead of waiting three or four days I returned the very next morning to the station, much to the surprise of the officers. It was just as I had expected. Quite a number of horses of a type far superior to those I had seen on the previous day were in evidence. The officers' faces plainly showed their embarrassment and they soon began to laugh. One of the captains said, with a grin:

"If this is the way you usually carry on, dear lady, you'll be able to take all the risks of your journey in your stride."

I pretended not to know what he meant.

"Why do you say that?" I asked him.

"Oh well, if you haven't noticed anything . . ."

"Well, I haven't—except that there are a few more horses here than there were before."

No one took me up on this quibble and I proceeded to examine the horses that interested me. Eventually I decided on a fine sorrel, four and a half years old, with a white streak on the forehead and white stockings on the hind legs. The stable description ran: 'Large white spot on forehead, continuing as streak to nostrils, between which it becomes dappled. Two large white patches on hind legs.' He was called Cachorro ('Cub') but I re-baptised him Young Luchador. I still needed a companion for him; by great good luck the head of the Civil Guard and Police, Don Arturo Zapata Velez, came to my rescue. He presented me with a second mount, a chestnut with a white star, seven years old.

As on the previous occasion, I had to embark on the work of training the animals for the journey ahead. It was an exhausting task in view of the short time available.

I presented Luchador to the Pinerolo Club, which had thoroughly deserved a gift from me and which was most grateful for the horse.

This club, the Pinerolo, I came to know well. Its merits entitle it to be known as the leading centre of horsemanship in South America; there ought to be many more such places. The club was founded by Count Eduardo Federico Morosini, professor of equitation, who had begun by establishing an Equestrian Academy in the beautiful grounds of the Lima Polo Club and thereafter converted his school into the great Racing Club which afterwards built up so eminent a reputation. I was deeply impressed by his exercising ground, his stables and the large number of horses he kept, particularly the superb thoroughbred Pinerolo, the pride and glory of the Academy.

The time I spent in the Peruvian capital allowed me leisure to inspect many of its chief sights and attractions, viewing it from the heights of the hill of San Cristobal, walking through its main streets, and standing before its great buildings. The cathedral is a magnificent edifice, containing the body of the daring conqueror from Estremadura, Francisco Pizarro. It is impossible here to give a description of the many churches, built in both the colonial and the modern style, such as those of San Francisco, Santo Domingo, and La Merced, which adorn the outskirts of the city, or to enumerate their treasures in detail, for Lima is one of the South American cities most splendid in its architecture. Few cities in Europe, even in Spain itself, surpass the majestic splendour of style exemplified by its churches. One becomes overawed in contemplation of the central nave of the cathedral or of the façade of San Agustin or of the gilded pulpit of the Old Church of the Magdalen.

It is not only the churches of Lima which uphold its reputation for colonial architecture; its other buildings alone render the city unforgettable. If it were not for the evidences of a vigorous modernisation in progress one might well believe that time had stood still here since the days when the Emperor Charles V called Lima the 'most noble and most loyal of cities'. I spent a long time admiring the former mansion of the marquesses of Torre Tagle, which now houses the Foreign Office.

This account of my ride must not be taken as a substitute for a guide to the cities of South America, but I cannot refrain from recording my most lasting impressions of them. It is easy to remember the great buildings of Lima, for they represent a summary of the history of the country from the time of Manco Capac, the Inca who presided over the glorious beginnings of the pre-Columbus empire, through Pizarro, who discovered it, and Bolivar and Marshal Sucre, who secured the independence of the colony, down to the heroes of the 2nd May, 1866, and Colonel Francisco Bolognesi, who made more recent history.

But historical and archaeological monuments tend to be lost in the modern urbanisation of Lima; lost in the many wide streets, such as the Alameda de los Descalzos, Arequipa Avenue which connects Lima with the splendid and colourful district of Miraflores, the Paseo de la Republica, the Paseo de Pierola and many other avenues and parks the names of which I have forgotten. But I still remember the Law Courts, the Government Palace, and the Ministry of Justice.

I stayed in Lima for a month and twenty-four days, which was the minimum time required to complete my legal business and the training of the horses. I left with the mare Pobre India, Young Luchador and Fury, my third horse, who, though very strong, active, and good-tempered, had one drawback: he had not been fully castrated and was therefore liable to be a nuisance.

We had no sooner left the Peruvian capital behind than it became clear that progress was going to be terribly difficult. The heat grew more and more oppressive and the animals began to suffer from sunstroke. They kept stopping, showed signs of fatigue and panted heavily. At times they lay down and I had the greatest difficulty in inducing them to rise. The sun's rays poured down like molten lead. The road ran alternately over sand and rocks, for I had now entered the mountainous coastal region, with its sandy beaches stretching down to the sea. Rocky hills and sand succeeded one another with monotonous regularity. I took refuge from time to time in fishermen's cottages. All four of us endured agonies of thirst. Whenever I could get enough water to bathe the animals' heads I used it all up for that purpose, though I would have given anything for a drink myself.

Horses deserve all we can do for them. They are prodigal of their strength and their blood for our benefit, though they are also very free with their blood for the benefit of mosquitoes, which attack them for days and nights on end. Their intelligence has always been underestimated, in common with their instinctive comprehension of matters which could never be explained to them. For example, at one place along that mountainous coast the fishermen employed a certain method of distilling salt water. After treatment in this fashion it could be drunk by human beings with little or no distaste. But the horses naturally did not understand that the water had been distilled and would never touch it.

The problem of food, though acute, was less troublesome than that of water. At that period carob beans and maize-leaves were all I could provide for their main diet.

I passed through endless villages, towns or stations of the Civil Guard. Some, like Trujillo, were fine old colonial settlements of considerable prosperity. Yet my journey continued to be wearisome and even monotonous owing to the unvarying character of the landscape. Nevertheless, it was not completely uninteresting; the grandeur of Andean scenery lingers vividly in the memory of a traveller long after he has left it. The convenience and facilities of life in large cities never console him for its loss once he has feasted his eyes on the spectacle of those menacing but majestic surroundings, so full of implacable strength.

The last few days of my ride through Peru seemed as though they would never end; I was always being told that a village or a station was quite near and always finding it at greater and greater distances across the wilderness. Sometimes I rode forty or more miles in a day, which was about as much as one could expect the horses to do, and to have made a habit of it would have worn them out.

I cannot complain, in general, of the treatment I received from the Indians. They were accommodating enough if one bears in mind their utter indifference to practically everything that goes on around them. It is hard to break through the icy crust of this apathy. For every twenty questions the whites or those of mixed blood asked me the aboriginals would ask me one or two. At some isolated dwellings I believe that if it had not been for the horses hardly anyone would have troubled to ask me where I was going or where I had come from. These people are so incurious by nature that one would suppose them to be eternally meditating on some private matter of great moment, as they incessantly chew their coca-leaves, the magical drug that apparently enables them to survive and forget their troubles. It is said that in the days before Columbus the coca-leaf was reserved for the use of the Inca or sovereign ruler and the most important of the officials, but the habit of chewing it had already grown common by the period of the Spanish conquest and the plant was then found everywhere. It had been considered divine in ancient times, so much so, indeed, that the wife and sister of Mayta Capac was given the name of Mama Coca in addition to the title of descendant of the Sun.

Heat and humidity, the climate that prevails on the eastern slopes of the Andes, some 6,500 feet above sea-level, are the most favourable conditions for the cultivation of the coca-plant. Its berry is only used as seed. The bush, with its thickly clustering leaves, may grow to a height of over five feet and live for thirty or forty years. The harvesting of the leaves, which takes place three times a year, and their drying are the two most important stages in production, the drying being a highly developed technique. In the old days, when the Indians were slaves and subject to forced labour, cultivation of the coca-plant was deliberately speeded up to prevent the swarms of unfortunate labourers in the mines from pining away and so as to keep them busy and active. The intensification of this labour for purposes of profit and the impossibility of forbidding the aboriginal to chew the leaf then formed a vicious circle. I have seen many people who are not aboriginals and consider themselves quite civilised, yet cannot break themselves of the habit.

The worst thing about that coast road is its stifling heat. The liability of the horses to sunstroke which I have already mentioned increased to an alarming extent; my own throat burned like fire and cracks appeared in my skin.

Many Chinese fishermen lived along the coast and for days on end I ate nothing but fish. Fresh water became very scarce and I suffered agonies of thirst. In some districts water was almost worth its weight in gold and it was a great day when I met a lorry carrying supplies of it and was able to obtain a little. However, despite my torments I had the compensation of observing nature in terrifying splendour; on one side of me stretched the vast plain of the Pacific Ocean and on the other the massive, undulating ramparts of the Andes.

As one travels further into the north of Peru, towards the frontier of the country, the tribes and communities of aboriginals seem deeper rooted in their changeless and poverty-stricken existence, making them indifferent, apparently, to their lack of resources, unless their unconcern is due to a wise contempt for ambition. But this trait and everything else that a rider such as myself may notice, especially what continues to survive of the old primitive ways, is subject to change, and change is, in fact, nearly always taking place. A traveller can only record what he sees close at hand. He neither knows nor troubles himself about what may be happening thirty miles to his right or left.

This reflection is peculiarly applicable to a characteristic and disagreeable feature of life in Peru, its earthquakes. Importance is only attributed to those which affect the district in which one happens to be. I had already, while staying at the house of Count Eduardo Morosini in Lima, experienced a few shocks of this kind, though they were not serious. All the same, the moment I felt my bed oscillating as if it were being shaken by a movable platform, I leapt out of it as nimbly as a hare and dashed into the street half-dressed, long before the other occupants of the house appeared, as indeed they did a few minutes later. They were not, however, quite so frightened as I was, as they had had a good deal of practice in gauging the proportions of an earthquake. I need not add that their experience was not much use to them when a real catastrophe occurred.

In the course of my ride to the Peruvian frontier I actually beheld, with something like real panic, a real earthquake in the mountains. Just before it happened, the horses showed signs of distinct uneasiness as though something in the air was worrying them. As I always kept a sharp eye on any movement, however casual, of the animals, I noticed at once that they felt something was wrong though I could not imagine what it was. An Indian who had joined me on the road— he grew coca-plants on a tiny allotment—halted abruptly, raising his head to sniff the wind exactly like a hunting dog.

"Bad, that's bad," he said, turning to me.

"What do you mean?" I asked.

For answer he lay down and put his ear to the ground. He got up with a very serious expression on his face and a single word on his lips.

"Earthquake."

He advised me, refusing to listen to any discussion of the matter, not to go a step further. It was not very clear to me what he was talking about and as I had a rooted aversion to unnecessary delays I tried to proceed on my way, clapping heels to my horse and taking no more notice of the Indian.

The latter planted himself in front of the animal as if he would rather be trampled underfoot than let it move. The horses themselves, moreover, as I did not fail to observe, seemed reluctant to go on. Well, I thought, the advice of a local inhabitant and the instinct of an animal combined are worth complying with, so I stayed where I was.

These events occurred in much less time than it has taken to describe them. Next moment a dreadful rumbling sound met our ears as though thunder were rolling beneath our feet. A whole huge peak which we could see quite plainly began to tremble. Rocks, followed by a few huge boulders, started rolling down its sides. I dropped to the ground and so did the Indian. We were near the path of an appalling landslide, the ultimate extent of which I could not guess. We had a perfect view of the earthquake from where we lay. But the look on the Indian's face calmed my apprehensions a little. It was evident that his experience led him to believe that we should have little to fear if we did not move from our position.

The phenomenon did not last long, though it appeared to me to do so. When at length we could safely proceed on our way we had the greatest difficulty in finding the road, which had completely disappeared under the rocks which had fallen on it, until we had left the zone affected by the earthquake behind.

The horses continued to show signs of panic, shying and losing their footing several times. While we were lying on the ground I had done my best to keep them near me by holding on tight to their bridles. But during my momentary terror and their own they jerked the reins violently out of my hands and made off at full gallop as though they had gone mad. Even with the Indian's help I had great difficulty in catching them afterwards.

After this adventure and others less sensational I arrived at Tumbes and Aguas Verdes, on the frontier between Peru and Ecuador.

CHAPTER X

HUNTERS AND BEASTS OF PREY

O N reaching the frontier the first thing I did was to get
rid of Pobre India. The mare had been more of a
hindrance than a help to me and I had found the pro-
vision of food for her a strain. I left her on loan, or rather by
way of a souvenir, for I had no idea of taking her back,
with a Canadian lady who lived close to the frontier.

After disposing of my ballast in this fashion I set out to
enter Ecuador. I found the formalities of obtaining a visa
desperately slow. I had been told in Peru that I should have
to be careful how I handled those 'monkeys', as the Peruvians
called their Ecuadorian neighbours, who returned the compliment by calling the Peruvians 'chickens'. These interchanges
might be witty enough, but my only concern was to get leave
to continue my journey.

Horses were not being allowed to enter Ecuador on account
of an outbreak of foot-and-mouth disease. I wore out my
lungs in the attempt to convince the authorities that I and
my two horses formed a single entity, not to be separated.
No use—I was told that my only chance would be to take the
animals by sea from Puerto Bolivar to Guayaquil. There seemed
no help for it. Despite my violent protests to the inspectors
they declined to entertain any other proposal. I left the horses
in quarantine and embarked alone on the small vessel plying
between the two places mentioned. In Guayaquil the authorities
insisted on the horses being brought to the city by sea. The
voyage from Puerto Bolivar was very short, but I was unwilling
to cover even a mile of my journey dismounted. Nevertheless,
it proved impossible, owing to the epidemic, to ride the horses
into the country and I was obliged, after doing all I could to

persuade the authorities to see my point, to fetch the animals into Guayaquil by sea. While they were being embarked at Puerto Bolivar Young Luchador slipped on the loading-platform, which had been faultily adjusted and was lying at a slant. He took what seemed to be a bad tumble but fortunately the consequences were not serious.

On arrival in Guayaquil I set myself to treat him for the bruises sustained in the fall. For eight days I could get neither him nor his companion anything to eat but jujube-tree cuttings. My faithful steeds were fated to subsist at times on all sorts of fodder. Often they were obliged to swallow the leavings of meals from military messes and other official establishments, as though they were literally beggars.

From Guayaquil to Vince I rode alongside the river Daule, the Pula, the Vince and through the town of that name, as far as Quevedo, some fifty miles further on, through very wild, mountainous country, with river crossings that proved equally troublesome and dangerous.

I had heard a lot about the great heat prevalent throughout Ecuador but between Guayaquil and Quevedo I found the temperature really quite agreeable. All I had to contend with was the fording of the rivers which lay across my path. It is true that on their banks, at suitably deserted spots, I was able to perform the indispensable operation of washing my clothes and laying them out to dry in the sun but sometimes it was quite a job crossing those rivers.

At one place a ferry was run by the municipality, theoretically free of charge. But the men employed to look after it demanded a hundred Ecuadorian pesos for the crossing. This was a sum I could not afford. Accordingly, I decided to embark, with the horses, in a canoe paddled by a boy, who good-naturedly offered to take us. I unsaddled the animals and stripped them of their harness for the crossing, intending to go back for these impedimenta afterwards.

It was difficult for the horses to keep their footing in the canoe. Young Luchador fidgeted incessantly. In one of his restless movements he fell overboard dragging the boy, who had been trying to keep him quiet, with him. I had quite a

struggle to prevent the pair of them being drowned. This
incident occurred a few miles before we reached Vince. I
had an equally bad time getting the poor animals across the
great river Quevedo, where there was a wooden pontoon
bridge with slatted decking, on which the animals kept
slipping. In the end they crossed more by swimming than
by anything else. I had been warned that there were only two
roads, one being the haunt of brigands and the other that of
beasts of prey; I decided to take the second road. It is fair
to record that I didn't meet any brigands at that time. But
I did meet the wild animals. The most dangerous of the latter
in that part of the world is the 'tiger', a word constantly on
the lips of the local population. This brute is really the jaguar.
It is very strong and active, though not as agile or as big as
the true tiger, but its strength is prodigious and it has a
most awe-inspiring roar.

The first time I saw it my heart almost froze with terror.
The whole thing happened very quickly. The hair of the
horses' hides bristled. They came to a sudden halt, trembling
all over. We were descending a slope between hills when,
with a loud crackling and rustling of bushes and foliage, a
fantastic pair of animals burst into the open.

The larger was a creature of the cattle species. I don't
remember whether it was a bull of the type familiar to me;
it may have been some kind of buffalo. The smaller animal
was the jaguar. It had mounted on the back of its prey and was
tearing furiously with its claws at the other beast's throat.
The latter was galloping in a mad frenzy, as though the devil
were after it. The 'tiger' was a magnificent creature, with
a glossy hide that gleamed like velvet. The markings covered
the brilliantly golden skin with very regular shapes, like
a decorative design. The head gave an impression of great
solidity and power, while the body and limbs suggested
irresistible muscular strength.

They flashed across the road like a thunderbolt and vanished
into the thickets of the hill on the other side. Soon afterwards I heard a pathetic, pitiable bellowing. The jaguar had
made its kill and the victim was yielding up its life.

With President Somoza of Nicaragua.

With Indians of Guatemala at the festival of San Pedro Nectar.

With Indians of Guatemala in mid festival and mime.

I decided to stay where I was and resort to the method which, as I had always heard, was generally employed to keep such beasts of prey at a distance. The idea was to light a big fire and remain close to it, waiting to see whether, by good fortune, other travellers might come along. If several persons were present the risk would be less.

I set to work to collect dry wood, of which there was plenty about, and had soon managed to kindle a good blaze, by which time the afternoon had waned and night was falling.

My chief worry was the danger to the horses, which were as nervous as I was myself. Their trembling, restless movements never ceased for an instant.

I stayed awake all night beside the fire with my two companions. Just before dawn one of the local people arrived. I think he was a forester. He was surprised to see me sitting by such a big fire, which the prevailing temperature hardly warranted. I explained what had happened.

The man's features showed that he lived in almost constant terror of the 'tigers'. After hearing my story, he seemed more frightened than ever. At that very moment the characteristic formidable roar of the animal rang out. The peasant assured me that it had been made by a pair of jaguars in company.

His anxiety was now turning to positive panic and he proceeded to make to me the most dreadful suggestion that I have ever heard. When I realised what he meant I felt like taking my whip to him.

His proposal was more or less to this effect. As the jaguar's favourite prey is an animal of the horse type, one way for the two of us to escape would be to tie up one of my horses as bait, put out the fire as quickly as we could and make off on the other one.

I gave him the rough edge of my tongue, though he had no idea why. He had himself told me that he knew a place close by where some hunters were camping out in the mountains. I did my best to convince him that if he went there on foot, without taking so great a temptation to a jaguar as a horse, he could make the journey with little or no risk. He could then tell the hunters to come at once and get us all out of our jam.

At last I succeeded in persuading him to make the attempt. He returned shortly afterwards, accompanied by two of the hunters, who were armed with modern rifles. I guessed that the business of these gentry might not be exclusively hunting, but in my perilous situation I did not care in the slightest what their business might be.

While they were talking to me, expressing their surprise at finding me there and congratulating me on my project as well as drawing up a plan of campaign to shoot the jaguars, Fury, with a frantic shake of his head, broke loose from his tether and galloped off down the road like a mad thing. Before we had time to think how to stop him a huge jaguar also leapt into the road. No doubt it was the same animal I had seen before, which had been stalking the horses.

Fury redoubled his speed, as though challenged on the race-track, and the jaguar tore after him in great bounds, gaining on him fast. I felt like covering my eyes; I foresaw the leap with which the brute would spring on Fury's crupper or back to claw the poor beast to death with those terrible forepaws.

At that moment both hunters levelled their rifles and fired. The sound of the shots seemed to surprise the jaguar, which immediately ceased its pursuit of the horse and began moving very slowly, with immense caution, gathering itself together at intervals and dragging itself along the road. The hunters fired again and the animal darted into the thickets of the mountain-side. We saw that it had left a trail of blood behind; it had obviously been hit.

The hunters and the Indian helped me to recapture Fury but it was some hours before we eventually caught him. We then all moved on together for some twelve miles, till I took leave of my escort. I determined to procure the best rifle I could find at the earliest opportunity.

Beyond Quevedo the heat closed down on us once more. I suffered so much from indigestion that I could hardly stand. Fury also fell very sick. He suddenly dug all his four feet into the ground and nothing could make him go on. He was sweating and breathing heavily. It was true that he had not eaten for two days and two nights. But I did not believe that hunger alone could be responsible for his present condition. It was necessary to do something. I took off his saddle and harness and hid them among some large bushes. He lay down and began snorting very hard. A number of the local inhabitants of all ages came to my assistance and between us all we managed to push and pull Fury as far as the nearest hut. These helpful Indians also knew where to find some jujube-trees, which they cut up with their *machetes* (large knives) for the horses to eat. The animals devoured them very eagerly. I borrowed a *machete* myself and threw myself with energy into the task of cutting more.

The problem of feeding the horses would now be much less troublesome, for we were already in the midst of the banana-growing district and the animals would soon get used to eating nothing but bananas.

Eventually Fury got over his fit of faintness, thanks largely to the attentions of the Indians. What I had thought might be a fatal seizure now left him, though I did not consider it advisable to move him for the time being. I recovered his saddle and harness and rode on to Esperanza mounted on Young Luchador.

While I was absent from Esperanza, having gone back to fetch the other horse, thieves stole practically all the clothing I had packed in my canvas bag. This was a deplorable misfortune for me, as in that part of the world it was extremely difficult for me to replace what I had lost, quite apart from the fact that I had to economise my resources very strictly.

I had been waylaid by robbers, but in the meantime my horses had also been attacked, and by one of their most cruel enemies, tick fever. Both were infected and no means existed anywhere in that district for eradicating the ticks that caused the disease. Both animals suffered visibly from the ravages of the parasites and Fury's recovery from his former illness was delayed. The veterinary surgeon at Pilalo bled him, thus affording him some relief. I was told at this place that the road ahead would be troublesome and the lieutenant in charge of the troops stationed there decided to provide me with an escort. It was a holiday in the town and the Indians were coming down from the highlands to take part in the festivities, the women wearing their best pointed hats and the men their most gaudy cloaks.

I was able to see an Indian wedding in Pilalo. It was a simple and picturesque ceremony. The rite took place in a candle-lit room filled with men muffled in cloaks who did not utter a word.

The priest asked the bridegroom: "How old are you?"

The bridegroom replied with another question: "How old should I be?"

The two contracting parties worked out his age as best they could, by recalling the number of harvests he had seen and the length of time various domestic animals had lived. The local magistrate then fixed the date of birth.

Next he enquired: "How many children have you?"

I was rather surprised by this question. But from the calm, official tone in which it was put I supposed that the magistrate had some definite reason for asking it.

"Four," replied the Indian. A note was taken of his answer and the benediction was then pronounced.

The governor of the district sent for the Indians who had come down from the mountains and picked out twenty of both sexes. He then told them:

"You will accompany this lady, who is a foreigner and under the protection of the Government. You will be responsible for her safety and will not leave her until she reaches the next town and is well supplied with everything she needs to continue the journey she has so courageously undertaken."

The Indians proclaimed in chorus that they would carry out his orders and take as good care of the traveller as of their own lives. They agreed in so many words to guarantee my arrival at the next place on my route, Sumbahua.

The intervening territory was of such a rugged and forbidding nature that the governor, or officer in charge of the Indian population, declared his conviction that I should never be able to cross it without the aid of the numerous escort he had provided. The region being mountainous, with no roads except the tracks made by the Indians, my companions were obliged to exercise continuous control over the horses, as their hoofs slipped every moment on the rough surface of the paths. We must have looked like a small battalion engaged in the mad attempt to lug a couple of big animals over impracticable country. Every time the horses jumped they risked a fall over some precipice. Prodigious efforts were needed to climb the steeper heights. I had to resort to every expedient I could think of to prevent my escort from losing heart. It will be some time before I forget those days of travel, as we made for Quito.

I must explain, for the benefit of those who have had sufficient patience and curiosity to follow the stages of my route through the countries of South and Central America, that for a number of different reasons I was frequently obliged to take short cuts across country, abandoning the regular highways. Sometimes, on those occasions, I wished to save time by reducing the number of miles covered, so as to compensate for the long periods necessarily spent in certain capital cities. I was also often impelled to take this step because in many districts the highway or road ran on for miles and miles in utter solitude, where it was impossible, at the average speed maintained by the horses, to find anywhere to pass the night or obtain supplies.

As for myself certain stages of my journey had already proved dangerous and were to prove so again, while others had been so lonely for such prolonged periods that I could not help feeling a certain amount of anxiety. One's fears are increased at night; I did my best to look like a man, wrapping myself up so as to disguise my appearance as far as possible, leaving only my boots and baggy trousers visible. I covered my hair and the lines of my figure, which might have betrayed my sex, as effectually as I could. If I heard footsteps in the distance and thought I might meet someone, I would light a cigarette. I only carried such things on me to enable me to perform this trick. As I don't smoke, I did not enjoy the experience, but muffled up as I was and showing light from the glowing end of the cigarette, as I drew in the smoke, no one would be likely to take me for a woman.

On reaching Latacunga I reported the theft of my clothing. The official whom I saw replied that he could take no steps to investigate the matter as Ecuador was an extremely democratic country and did not tolerate interference with the citizens.

"What would happen if I stole something myself, then?" The man shrugged his shoulders; I returned to the charge.

"Well, I also come from a democratic country—but I don't see why other people's property shouldn't be respected."

He intimated, as others had intimated to me before, that a bribe might work the oracle. I was not prepared to do this and, as he maintained his cynical attitude, I realized that for the moment it would be better to drop the subject.

All these difficulties were compensated for and forgotten when I reached the Avelina district, where the President, at that time Señor Gala Plaza, had a country house, a kind of ranch, where he spent his leisure. I was received by the President himself with true Ecuadorian hospitality, introduced to his wife and brother and lent a magnificent horse to ride on festive occasions. The Head of the State was living very simply on his ranch, plainly dressed in ordinary country clothes and surrounded by Indian servants who seemed devoted to him.

After my horses had been installed in perfect comfort the President asked me to give him some account of my adventures. A number of the Indians approached and begged their 'Dad', as they called him, to allow them to listen to my tale. Later on I was entertained at a meal presided over by the President's charming wife.

Among other festivities arranged in my honour I was present at a short bull-fight staged in one of the paddocks adjoining the estate. The President's brother, José Maria, was an enthusiastic adherent of the sport and talked learnedly of the various methods of conducting it, referring to the daring exponents of the art in Mexico and Spain. He mentioned

Arruza, Dominguin and Manolete, the latter, now dead, having been, he said, a positive prodigy and master of them all.

The bulls on this occasion had plenty of courage, for they had been brought from the highlands where ferocious herds of them were allowed to run wild. They were of so pure a mountain breed that some of them fell ill and died of chagrin when they were removed from the hills.

In talking with the President I told him what had been said to me about Ecuador being a 'democratic country' when I reported the theft of my clothes. He laughed heartily at the story and promised me that the State would make good all my losses. He offered me two spirited horses to ride while those I had brought with me were resting. Young Luchador and Fury were afterwards sent to the capital, Quito, and when I arrived there a great entertainment was given in my honour; athletic sports were held on the football field in the presence of a large crowd of spectators and the whole affair proved a great success. My horses subsequently returned to Señor Plaza's ranch and remained there during the twenty-two days I stayed in the capital.

While all these honours were being paid to me I received a communication from the Treasury stating that I had violated Ecuadorian law by introducing horses from abroad during the epidemic of foot-and-mouth disease. I showed the Treasury officials the papers I had obtained in Guayaquil and explained that I had arrived there by sea. In the end I was granted the favour, as I thought it, of a promise that when my horses arrived I would be given papers relating to them which would prevent any further interference. A petition signed by fifty Ecuadorians also guaranteed payment of the fines to which I was liable. I declined, however, to take advantage of this offer and paid the fines myself.

Eventually, faithful to my unvarying motto of 'Forward!', I took leave of the agreeable city of Quito and its admirable inhabitants. Whatever the future might hold, I thought, at least my horses had enjoyed a good rest.

I also found the city of Ibarra, which I visited subsequently, very agreeable. Here Señor Bolivar E. Almeida, Clerk to the

Province of Imbabura, wrote in my day-book: 'I hereby certify that Señorita Ana Beker, of Argentine nationality, visited the city of Ibarra on her way to the countries of the North. She left us with a profound appreciation of her wide culture and attractive personality.'

I was now approaching the frontier of Colombia and about to take leave of yet another of the lands lying on my route through the vast and varied extent of the continent of South America.

At Tulcan, the last town on my road through Ecuador, I made the acquaintance of a certain colonel, in charge of that region, who added to my favourable impressions of the good nature of his compatriots. The only trouble with him was that whenever I addressed him I always had to start with "Say, Colonel——" If I didn't do so he said I didn't sound as though I came from Argentina. It is a curious fact that in a number of places in South America they refer to the Argentines as the 'Says'.

At Tulcan I engaged a small room in an Indian lodging-house in which to pass the night. That evening I went for a walk with some of the local girls, accompanied by the police-surgeon. I took with me the key of the padlock securing the door of my room. Nevertheless, when I returned I saw the door standing open.

"What's this?" I enquired. "Has someone gone in there?"

"Yes, there's a little chap sleeping there," replied the innkeeper, and sure enough, big or little, there he was, snoring away beside my bed.

I protested vigorously.

"But that's my cousin," the innkeeper told me.

"I don't care who he is," I retorted. "He's got to clear out of here this instant if you don't want me to start a row that'll be heard at the police station."

And they lugged the little fellow, bed and all, at top speed, into the cold night air.

CHAPTER XI

A COLOURED SCARF

COLOMBIA was in sight. I entered the country by way of
Ipailes, where I was able to inspect the picturesque
Lajas shrine. Thence I proceeded to Pasto, lying at
the foot of the volcano of Galeras; in spite of this town's
name my horses could not find a square yard of grazing anywhere and they had to be content with the remains of the
evening meal served to the troops in the barracks.

Pasto is the capital of the department of Marino, and strongly
resembles the towns of its neighbour, Ecuador. I rode through
Buesaco to La Union along a barren road flanked by occasional
stunted trees. While we were passing a train of mules one
of them gave Young Luchador a hard kick high up on the
foreleg. Unfortunately inflammation set in on the cut
to such an extent that I had to consult a veterinary
surgeon.

The mayor of La Union told me that there was no vet
in the town; fortunately, however, there was a doctor.
I would have much preferred a vet, but I was obliged, in
the circumstances, to accept, though with reluctance, the
treatment and advice proffered by the medico. The latter's
features bore a half cynical, half sympathetic smile as he
watched me talking to the patient.

"What's the matter, boy? Tell me," I pleaded.

The horse answered with a pitiful neigh.

"Where does it hurt? Can't you tell me that?"

He whinnied again, stretching out his painful foreleg.

"It's an infection," I told the doctor imploringly.
"External treatment won't be any good."

"Let me remind you that I am a doctor," he said with a

frown. "I'm doing you a favour by prescribing at all for a sick animal."

He recommended the application of an ointment, but I insisted that a mere daubing of the sore would be useless. I added:

"I believe the only cure would be several millions of units of penicillin."

Eventually the doctor gave in, shrugging his shoulders. "It's your horse and it'll be your penicillin, if you can buy or beg any of the stuff."

Luck was in my way; I managed to obtain enough of the drug to give the animal a dose which could well be called 'strong as a horse'. The progress of the infection was retarded sufficiently to enable us to continue our journey. I rode on with a good deal of misgiving, for I had been told that the road from La Union to Patia was infested by a band of ferocious blacks, practically outlaws. Some days before, they had murdered a travelling salesman and his wife simply to rob them of their modest stock in trade.

I released the safety-catch of my revolver and kept it handy for instant use in case I was surprised.

As on such occasions one's fears nearly always turn out to have been exaggerated, I did not believe I was going to be easily caught napping. But I was, though it could not really have been called a surprise, as I had been thinking of nothing else ever since the warning.

Four half-naked blacks came out on to the road and demanded in loud, harsh voices to know where I was going and what I had to sell.

I answered them at a gallop, for before I uttered a word I had already spurred my horse. They ran after me as hard as they could. The road was narrow, with a rough surface and a steep upward gradient; the horses could not develop much speed and one of the blacks managed to get hold of the tail of the pack-horse. The animal shook off his grasp with a violent movement and at the same time launched a few well-aimed kicks which bowled the assailant over and left him lying in the road. I had no intention of going to his assistance and rode on as before, constantly looking over my shoulder, with levelled revolver, in case there should be a chance of planting a shot in the white, or rather in the black, if I may be forgiven the joke. I think that the horse's kicks saved me from a very real danger, for I remember that the fellow they sent spinning had a sharp knife in one hand when he caught the animal's tail in the other; it is quite possible that he meant to hamstring the horse, which would have been as good as slaughtering it.

The negro region extended as far as El Bordo. On the road to that place I saw a number of other coloured people, who passed the time of day with me quite peacefully and there were no other attempted attacks.

Immediately after this stage of my journey the sorrel began to show signs of very serious ill-health. He was suffering from a kind of acute itch, which caused him to scratch and wallow in the most frantic fashion, tearing away strips of his flesh and hide. I was told that the irritation was produced or communicated by a certain plant. In any case the stifling heat and the frightful exasperation caused by the itching had reduced the poor animal to a pitiable condition.

We passed through Popayan, a town where many exquisite gems of architecture, in the colonial style, have been preserved, such as the Church of Santo Domingo. The climate is excellent, with an average temperature of 64 degrees, and the atmosphere of the ancient Spanish tradition has been maintained ever since the foundation of the town by Sebastian de Belalcaza. I should have preferred to be in a better mood to appreciate such relics of the past, but I was worried to the point of obsession about the state of my horses, especially that of Young Luchador. His belly had swollen to such an extent that it had become a monstrous appendage. In a frenzy of anxiety I searched for veterinary surgeons all over the place. The few I found could do little or nothing to reduce the swelling. I was at my wits' end. A malign fate appeared to be persecuting my horses. Yet I had always taken the greatest pains to keep them in health. Whenever I came across water anywhere I invariably gave them a bath, soaping and scrubbing, till I was exhausted, the parts affected by the itch or the tick fever. This last pest was by no means confined to the horses. It several times attacked my own person. I would not wish my worst enemy to suffer from it. There is a small variety of tick which bores its way into one's skin, causing a fearfully painful smarting and itching that drives one nearly mad.

My torments were destined to be prolonged until I eventually discovered, thanks to the advice of some half-breeds I met at a farm, the way to counteract the depredations of this parasite: the remedy is to rub oneself practically all over with pigs' fat. The trouble I had, after I had been told about this wonderful and much needed remedy, to find enough of it to daub my horses and myself may be imagined.

As for the alarming state of Young Luchador, the groom at the headquarters of the mounted police in the last town I came to offered to solve the problem.

"If you'll trust me," he said, "I can guarantee to cure your horse provided you'll do what I tell you."

I had tried everything, so I had no choice but to let him carry on. The groom instructed me to tie the animal's forefeet together. Then, with a razor-blade, he made a number of cuts in the horse's belly. A purulent liquid began to drip from the cuts. Penicillin was then applied and a week later Young Luchador could be considered out of danger.

Having been preoccupied with anxieties of this kind and concerned solely with the continuance of my ride, I had not been paying any attention to the political disturbances agitating the country through which I was travelling; I was soon rather rudely awakened to the realities of the political situation.

I happened to be riding along deep in thought when I met a lorry full of armed men who were all talking at once at the top of their voices, apparently in a great state of excitement. They no sooner caught sight of me than someone gave an order for the lorry to pull up, whereupon its occupants started cross-examining me in disagreeably bullying fashion.

"Are you a liberal?"

In my astonishment at this question I took it literally and answered:

"Yes, I think I'm quite a liberal sort of person——"

"You belong to the Liberal Party?" They fairly yelled at me this time.

Their furious attitude gave me little time for reflection. "I don't belong to any party," I said. "I'm a traveller and an Argentine. How can I possibly know what you're talking about?"

"What are you wearing that red scarf for, then?"

It was true that I was wearing a red woollen scarf. I couldn't know that it might be taken for a sign that I belonged to a certain political group and might therefore let me in for trouble.

"All right then," I said. "If my scarf annoys you so much give me another in exchange for it, any colour you like."

At this retort the lorry-load of busybodies drove off. But a little further on I met another. Its occupants, no doubt for the same reason as that for which the first lot had stopped me, started pelting me with green bananas for all they were worth. They smashed a cork-crowned hat I was wearing and bruised me all over with their missiles. My horse shied under this rain of projectiles and spilled me in the ditch.

At the first village I entered some women told me I had better find out in advance, wherever I went, which party, Liberal or Conservative, dominated the situation in that district. As the Conservatives wore blue, it would be as well to provide myself with a scarf of that colour.

I rode on, encountering the usual difficulties and problems, through the towns of Santander, Palmira, Buga, Tulua and other less important places on my route. I turned off the road to pay a visit to Cali, on the river Cauca, a beautiful modern city with a large population and many tourists. Situated at well over 3,000 feet above sea-level, the place has an international airfield and there is also a great deal of traffic along the Cauca. The population is about 200,000. I stayed at Sevilla for the New Year festivities.

Another year had passed. My plans were gradually coming

to fruition. I had made quite satisfactory progress, on the average; I felt I could be content. Nevertheless, I had miles and miles still to cover. On any map they looked positively endless. My journey was by no means completed.

I had crossed the towering ridges of a massive mountain range and the picturesque Cauca valley. Everything would have been quite simple if it had not been for the political revolution in progress. After the death of Señor Gaitan, which caused a considerable stir all over the country, passions ran high and grievances were aired by shooting in the streets of the towns and even in the rural districts.

All the same, the only trouble I had at that time was the delay I experienced in consequence of the mistake made by a blacksmith. He had not, 'struck the quick' of my horse's hoof, but fitted an extremely small shoe on him, with the result that three days later the animal went lame. I had to detach these shoes and turn the horse out to grass for a whole week, to give his hoofs time to grow. After that I had him reshod.

I set out for Bogotá along a very difficult mountain road which did not get any easier and had to be negotiated very slowly. In some villages I heard the curfew tolling and re-membered that a merciless civil war was raging. At one place, near the railway, a statue had been erected in memory of Gaitan. A hail of bullets was directed upon it from a passing train but some hours later, in the early evening, a procession of people passed in front of the statue and laid flowers at its foot.

At Bogotá I received a great welcome; the Press and those in the know had spread the news of my arrival.

I stayed eight days in the capital of Colombia, during which I was able to admire the many splendid treasures of this great city. Always followed by a multitude of inquisitive and wondering spectators, I rode up the Avenue of the Centenary, crossing the wide, handsome squares, and paused to contem-plate the magnificently spacious Plaza Bolivar, the capitol, and University City. I also much enjoyed excursions by the funicular railway to Montserrate and visits to the Bolivar

Estate, as well as strolls along the streets of houses dating from colonial days.

I shall long remember this great South American centre, which has never ceased its progressive career since its foundation by Gonzalo Jimenez de Quesada. I also rode a few miles out of the city to visit the Tequen Falls on the river Bogotá, a perpendicular drop of about 475 feet, resembling a huge curtain of foam in its roaring descent over the rocks. An old Indian woman told me that if you look hard at the foam you can see mirrored in it the head of Bochica, either a god or a human benefactor of the aboriginal race inhabiting the Bogotá highlands.

The people I met were most cordial and their standard of culture was particularly high. There seemed to be a great many poets, a race to which some have referred facetiously as a pest, but which in reality has a great deal of wit and sensibility. I have kept a number of the poems which were dedicated to me and in particular one by a student whom I met at a party.

There was much less poetry about the tedious proceedings involved in obtaining the documents necessary to cross into Panama. I ran into the whole weight of rigid obstruction characteristic of officials who invariably apply the same measure to all the laws they administer. Payment was demanded in advance for both the outgoing and the return journey and I also had to fulfil further requirements which proved an utter lack of understanding on the part of officialdom of the point of a ride like mine. A letter from the Argentine ambassador guaranteeing my departure from Panama on the expiry of my visa had some effect on the ultimate delivery of this document, though not until prodigious efforts and endless comings and goings had preceded its release.

In my ride from Sevilla to Bogotá I had crossed the country from west to east, beginning at Valle Colombia and then going on to the towns of Caicedonia, Calarca, Ibague, Oalanday, Flandes, Cundinamarca, Salto, and a few other such places, and I had also passed over the great Occidente Bridge on the 11th March, 1952.

From Bogotá to Medellin I travelled diagonally from east

to west, at an angle from the capital. I passed places like Villeta, Mariquita, which is called locally the centre of the Republic, and Manizales, the centre of the coffee-growing district, since most of this staple product of Colombian agriculture finds its way into that town.

The mention of such settlements throughout these pages may give the impression of a journey through territory dotted with small inhabited places. But for most of the time I was riding along extensive tracts of wilderness. The route to Medellin lay through one desolate region after another. It was very rough going all the way.

As I left the city I became aware that I was being followed by some horsemen; far from wishing to slacken my pace, I was anxious to accelerate it, as I gripped the butt of my revolver and wondered if something unpleasant were about to happen. But I decided to stop when I heard someone call out loudly behind me: "Rein those horses in if you don't want us to fire!"

When my pursuers came up I found they were police officers. They levelled their weapons at me and addressed me in harsh and menacing accents, which I thought very surprising.

"Pull up, there!" they shouted. "Right away, now!"

"Why?" I asked. "What have I done?"

"Where did you get those horses from?"

"A long way from here. Before I came to this country."

"Where did you buy them? Can you prove you bought them?"

"I was given them by high authorities acting on behalf of a certain Government."

They looked me up and down, hard. Then one of them said:

"What have *you* got to do with authorities and Governments?"

All this rumpus was due to the fact that two horses of the same colouring as mine had disappeared from the stables of the Mounted Police. I had great trouble in convincing my inquisitors of my identity. I had to show them all sorts of papers and documents, the signatures I had obtained and my newspaper cuttings.

As they turned away to leave me in peace, I said to one of them: "If you had listened to the radio or read the newspapers, you would have heard of my arrival and known who I was."

The man struck his forehead with his open hand: "Of course! It's that crazy woman who's going round the world with two animals for company!"

It was on the tip of my tongue to answer: 'Yes, and sometimes with two other animals behind!' However, I simply said: "So you think that's queer, do you?"

His companion cut in: "Once a woman makes up her mind she's capable of anything."

Then they both trotted back to the station.

As there were a great many rebels about, acting in defiance of the Government, I had various disagreeable encounters of this kind.

In Santa Barbara it seemed as though the previous episode was going to be repeated. I found myself at odds with an individual who might or might not have been a policeman, I couldn't be sure. He rode up to me on the public highway, told me he was an agent of the Colombian Police and said he was going to take me back with him in custody to Bogotá.

"I've no proof that you are a police officer," I objected. "I'm a foreigner. You can't give me orders."

His answer was to lay his hand on his revolver. But I was already covering him with mine.

It was true that he seemed to be wearing police uniform, though his tunic was unbuttoned and the belt carelessly fastened. But, as I told him when I took this defensive action, I was perfectly well aware that policemen had been killed in that district and their uniforms appropriated. I was able to keep him at bay for some time, during which he could not make up his mind what to do. Meanwhile some other persons arrived and asked me whether I had any complaints to make about the fellow's behaviour.

"No," I rejoined, for in the presence of this providential group of sensible people who seemed to have dropped from the sky I had quite regained my self-command. "No, he hasn't done anything. He's afraid to."

The newcomers told the unbuttoned one what they thought of him in no uncertain terms and some women who had joined the group abused him shrilly, with even greater indignation. They understood better than the men what he had been after and their hostile attitude made it clear that, though they had nothing against the civil war and the political murders that accompanied it, they disapproved of its being used as an excuse to interfere with foreigners or even natives, for that matter, who had nothing to do with it. Violent incidents of this kind, however, were becoming more and more frequent, reminding me that my little .38-calibre revolver was not very reliable. I decided that it would be necessary to obtain a really good one, as well as a rifle or shotgun. My encounters with wild beasts, and even with humans, had by this time convinced me that I ought to be well armed. I sold my revolver later on, when I entered Panama, replacing it with a remarkably fine one, and a box of ammunition.

At Medellin, those who welcomed and entertained me had a good deal to say about my intention of taking a short cut through the forests; I was told on several occasions that it would be madness for anyone, man or woman, to risk travelling through that bandit-infested jungle.

It was true that the term 'bandit' was used by both parties in the civil war to designate their antagonists, but there were men on both sides who did not hesitate to employ their weapons for the purpose of 'living off the country'.

Some of those people at Medellin who considered that I ran a great risk on account of my sex reminded me that the men hiding in the jungle had necessarily to abstain from women for long periods. They told me, for example, of a school-mistress whom the robbers had carried off to relieve the austerity of their lives and who had never been heard of again. I replied, with a laugh, that those who undertook journeys like mine and were determined to reach their destinations travelled under a special providence.

But it was only outwardly that I laughed. Nor did I laugh when I read, in one of the local Liberal newspapers, a eulogy of my wanderings and feats of endurance which sounded more like a speech at a funeral. 'Let us hope that the daring amazon will escape with her life,' wrote the author of the article. He proceeded to point out, at some length, that practically all those who had plunged into the forests in circumstances like mine had either disappeared for good or been found dead.

Though I soon abandoned Medellin, I did not abandon my enterprise; I spent only a short time in the town, which has a flourishing industry and considers itself to be the second most important city of the Republic. It contains a number of very active social and sporting clubs.

CHAPTER XII

THE JUNGLE

I REACHED the outskirts of the jungle soon after leaving
Medellin; it did not take me long to realize that my
previous idea of it as a mountainous, heavily timbered
and almost impenetrable region was so far from the truth as
to be almost ludicrous. The precipices and rocks of the
Andes had delayed our progress and even threatened to
engulf us in their chasms; but this appalling density of vegetation seemed to overwhelm and stifle us with its matted
tentacles. Once entangled in those formidable thickets,
there seemed to be little hope of ever emerging. The
difficulties of the terrain and the rank profusion of its plant
life grow steadily more forbidding. Its thorns, in perpetual
ambush, tear at one's clothing. Its trees rise to such a height
that the eye wearies of the strain of looking for their summits.
Their great boughs are inextricably intertwined with huge
ferns. The thickest limbs of the trees might be compared with
the arms of wrestling titans.

Other enemies of a much more insidious character are so
tiny that their attacks make a mockery of all defence. Thousands of insects of the most diverse varieties exasperated the
horses to such an extent with their stinging as almost to
deprive the animals of their reason. The poor animals, their
ears bristling, seemed to be expressing their fear that we
should never struggle out of that obstinate tangle of greenery.

The peculiarly oppressive character of forests is due to the
absence of any horizon. I did all I could to speed up the horses'
painful progress, for I was becoming more and more alarmed
at the utter lack of any traces of human habitation.

We covered twenty-five miles without seeing any living
creature apart from a few animals resembling foxes that crossed

our path and some forest birds that flew off screaming at our approach. I began to wonder whether we were lost for good.

As we were emerging from a path so narrow that the branches whipped my face and caught in the baggage carried by the packhorse I saw a tall, slender woman coming towards me. Her features were regular, though much tanned by exposure to the elements. She appeared to be about forty-five years old. There was something brisk and resolute about her aspect—not entirely surprising in a woman who evidently lived in the depths of the jungle.

She kept her eyes attentively fixed on me as I questioned her. I asked how far it was to the nearest house of any size. She answered that it was a good way, but that I could rest for a while in her hut if I cared to. She guided me to the hut, which stood in a small clearing where a few trees had been cut down. I gathered that she lived there alone with two or three cows. There was no bread in the place. She gave me a little maize-cake to eat. When night began to fall I sat down near the hut, after first seeing to my horses.

The woman was evidently struck by my pensive and melancholy expression. I was really feeling rather disheartened. Perhaps, I thought, those who had warned me it would be impossible to get through the woods had been right; I had already tempted fortune pretty often and now the outlook seemed very gloomy, for my resources by this time were running extremely low.

The woman touched my shoulder. "What's the matter?" she asked. "You look as if you were in trouble."

"Well, I suppose I am."

"Are you frightened?"

"What's the good of saying I'm not? I can't stop here and I'm told the jungle is full of bandits."

"You're afraid of them?"

"As you may imagine."

"Well, I'm their chief, you know." The woman drew herself up without ostentation and yet not without a certain pride.

"Is that true, or are you joking?"

"It's true."

I returned the only answer that, with my views, seemed appropriate in the circumstances.

"I must congratulate you. I think it would be a very good thing if women in general were all capable of holding such a position."

She told me that the so-called bandits were Liberal refugees, who were hiding in the woods.

As soon as the animals and myself were rested I told the female 'brigand chief' that I would have to go. She gave me some advice as to the road to follow and informed me which were the best catchwords to use among the rebels. She particularly warned me not to accept the escort of any Government troops, as the Liberal sharpshooters were hidden in the thickets and among the trees wherever they were least expected and would open fire on any uniformed Conservatives, as well as on anyone who accompanied such troops. She added that it would be best to continue my route alone and hatless so that I could be recognised as a woman and for that reason unlikely to be taking any part in hunting down the refugees.

I parted from this militant female 'bandit'—though she did not behave as a bandit to me—with a handclasp and went on through the tangled growths of the forest.

At the first military camp I came to the subaltern in charge offered me the escort of a few soldiers in view of the numerous bad characters he said were infesting the district. I declined with thanks, adding:

"I prefer to be alone. I know how to deal with these jungle bandits."

The lieutenant shrugged his shoulders, greatly astonished at my decision. One of his men said to me, as I was leaving:

"You're quite right. If we'd gone off in a crowd they'd have shot us all down. Those fellows hide like wolves and you never know where the next shot is coming from."

Apart from this risk of coming under Liberal fire, I should have been glad of the company of a few soldiers to help me cut my way through that endless jungle, which became almost impassable in some places.

I passed a spot where building of the Pan-American highway was going on. The men were not actually working on road construction, though they showed every sign of intense activity. One has to remember that the cutting of a road through country of that sort is a 'Roman job', as the popular saying has it. The first step has to be the felling of natural obstacles in that wild and intractable region.

For many days and nights after that I plunged on through, or rather buried myself in, those Colombian forests. In the Dabeiba and Uraba districts especially the going is about as bad as in any jungle in the world.

In those parts of the country the terrain became almost impenetrable. The compact mass of greenery, when seen near at hand and in detail, revealed a rich diversity of line and colour. I had to bend my head right back to catch a glimpse of an occasional small patch of sky, and there were long stretches when the heavens were quite invisible. The more massive of the trees seemed to be engaged in furious combat with their enormous boughs. The tangled, interlacing branches of the parasitic plants constrict and strangle the growth of the trunks with terrifying energy. One scarcely knows whether it is day or night, for the rays of the sun only occasionally strike diagonally through the thick foliage.

It was necessary to move very carefully, as otherwise one would lose sight of the narrow paths, one of which I found blocked by enormous tree-trunks. They seemed to have been felled at that spot in order to erect a strong barricade.

I had to dismount and help the horses over this obstacle with infinite toil and trouble. They continually fell to their knees and only scrambled up again after slipping repeatedly.

A shrill, terrified neighing from Young Luchador reminded me of other occasions when he had scented pumas or jaguars. At the same time the shrieking of the birds became deafening and I was sure it meant that large beasts of prey were in the neighbourhood. Jaguars often climb trees with much agility, causing panic among their feathered occupants.

On one occasion when I had wandered off the faintly marked track I heard a peculiar kind of low grunting or whining which I thought might be that of a fox or some similar creature. I searched the undergrowth and discovered a pair of jaguar cubs. They were playing with each other, rolling about and squealing, with the typically graceful movements of young animals of this species. For a moment I stood entranced, watching their harmless gambols. But Young Luchador and Fury did not appreciate the performance at all. They tugged at the reins and tried to back away, bending their hind legs. I saw so much terror in the eyes of the two horses that I concluded we were in imminent danger. Then I heard a thunderous roar. No doubt the mother of the cubs was approaching.

I realised at once that only the sound of the shots of my revolver, rather than its bullets, could save me. As a first step I resolved to get as far away as I could from the cubs.

But before I could do so I was interrupted. I heard a fearful roar and saw a jaguar bound, like a sentinel taking up position, onto a thick branch of the tree that stood nearest to the cubs, the horses and myself. There could be no doubt that it was the mother. She was a huge, powerfully built creature and it seemed to me that I could feel her snorting breath, despite the distance, on my very face. I could hardly expect anything else to happen but that the maddened animal, believing her whelps to be in peril, would immediately leap at us. Almost automatically, with no definite idea in my head, I fired the two cartridges I had left in the revolver. There was no time to reload.

The moment the two shots rang out they were re-echoed by what sounded like hundreds of others. A veritable hail of bullets whistled about my ears. They broke several of the branches close by. This crackling volley startled and frightened the jaguar. As for my horses, the mere sight of the beast had already paralysed them with terror. They stood huddled against each other, in a single, shuddering group.

As though all of us with one accord had decided to neglect everything but the urgent need to take cover from the fire that was apparently being directed against ourselves from some unknown ambush every one of the actors in this drama went into hiding. The jaguar left her branch for a less exposed position, half concealed in the tree's foliage, where she remained crouching as if in the hope of escaping observation. I myself succeeded in making the horses obey the usual calls to lie down and dropped to the ground in my turn.

It was high time we did so, for the firing started again. Though it was now less concentrated, it sounded much nearer. No doubt the jaguar instinctively longed to make off, but could not bring herself to do so in the continued presence of her cubs.

The thicket within which the whelps were lying parted and a group of men armed with rifles and shotguns appeared. They were followed by a number of others similarly equipped, till the entire body must have amounted to some forty or fifty persons. Several of them at once extended to form a small semi-circle, in advance of the main force, surrounding myself and the horses. They covered me with their weapons and seized the bridles of the animals. Between the two groups of men lay the cubs and above us in the tree the jaguar still crouched motionless.

One of the 'irregulars', as I called them to myself on account of their rough clothing, bandoliers and weapons, approached the jaguar cubs and struck them with the butt-end of his gun. They yelped shrilly and piteously. I did not know whether the men had yet noticed the mother. But to be on the safe side I pointed out where she was hidden, and shouted "Look out! Look out!" I was too late; in a flash the jaguar had gathered herself together and sprung, hurtling down with all her strength on the man who was striking at the cubs. Though she was but a single animal and there were many of the irregulars, her leap created such complete confusion at first that no effective assistance could be given to the man she had seized. He went down like a rag doll. I realised, with horror, that she would probably tear him to pieces in a few seconds. Then his companions came to his assistance. They slashed at the jaguar with their *machetes* and fired into the animal's body at close range, though it was difficult to take accurate aim owing to the risk of hitting the prostrate man.

This scene seemed to go on for hours. Actually it only lasted a moment or two. Then the 'tigress', riddled with bullets and bleeding from a dozen knife-wounds, lashed out with all four feet in her last furious death-agony and finally collapsed in the undergrowth. It seemed practically certain that her victim, too, would perish. He was carried away inert and covered with blood, his clothes torn to rags and one arm almost severed from his body where the jaguar's teeth had inflicted deep and fearful wounds.

I never knew what happened to him for he was taken away in a different direction from ours. I say 'ours' because I was also escorted from the spot by the armed guerrillas, who told me that I was to be formally examined with a view to finding out what I was doing in the jungle.

"You can take me anywhere you like and ask me any questions you please," I answered, "so long as you take care of my horses." The brigands, as I had generally heard them called, were encamped in a clearing of the forest.

The one who seemed to exercise most authority over the rest was a man of over sixty, with white, curly hair and by no means unpleasing features. He asked me a lot of questions. When I protested that I was a foreigner under the protection of my Government he retorted that he and his men were sick of Governments and their orders and that however admirable my project of a ride through America might be he would be obliged to detain me for the time being in the forest, as his men were determined that no one should be permitted to lay information or give any account whatever as to the situation of their camp or their proceedings in general.

"What do you mean by 'for the time being'?" I asked.

"Well, we shan't be in any hurry. You'll stay for as many days or months as may be necessary. Steps will be taken to provide fodder for your horses and you yourself will share our rations."

As may be imagined, the prospect of this enforced delay

for an indefinite period did not recommend itself to me. Desperate situations require desperate remedies, or so I have always heard. For the time being all I could do would be to hold my tongue and keep my own counsel. Though at the time I did not protest against my fate, I resolved nevertheless to try to escape. I realised that it would not be easy to do so among men actuated by such strong feelings and therefore naturally suspicious, but there wasn't the slightest chance of any other solution to the problem. I was counting on the advent of night to help me carry out my plan. But for some reason or other that night everyone stayed awake in a state of great excitement. Messengers came and went. Hardly any of the rebels slept a wink.

The next night, however, just the opposite happened. Almost everyone went to sleep and a deep silence reigned in the camp. I was not very closely guarded. The chief evidently thought he had convinced me by his argument that it would be utter madness for me to leave his community unless several men accompanied me.

While I remained with the irregulars I tried to improve my knowledge of the neighbourhood by asking questions about the forest paths and the location of such towns and villages as I had noted for my itinerary. 'Ask the way and you'll get to Rome,' is a common saying. But in that jungle, however persistently one enquired, there was always a grave risk of going astray.

Another proverb tells us that we are creatures of habit and can get used to the most extraordinary kinds of existence. During the previous stages of my ride I had grown accustomed to reaching one place after another by asking the way. However often I was temporarily lost or uncertain of my direction I always came in the end to where I wanted to be. Consequently, I came to believe that it would be the same in whatever barren wilderness I happened to find myself.

The day after my capture I took a stroll, accompanied by a few of the guerrillas, round the environs of the camp and tried to fix in my memory which would be the best way to ride for, anyway, three or four miles with both horses. I was the more anxious to rid myself of my protectors because I feared they had their eye on my animals. It is true, however, that when I caught one of the men giving them an appraising look and he noticed my expression of anxiety he told me they would not be much use to his companions owing to the extreme difficulty of controlling horses when taking cover.

I planned to escape on the following lines: as the irregulars did not possess horses with which to pursue me I would set mine off at a gallop down a certain path which I could see was relatively open. As soon as it ceased to be so I would try to get my bearings and make my way to the nearest village, thus continuing to put further miles of that long jungle ride behind me.

Accordingly, at midnight I secretly saddled the horses, without making them stand up and went off alone to the place where the path in question began. A low whistle that my equine friends understood very well was enough to cause them to rise and come slowly to meet me. I then mounted and put both animals into a fast trot. Soon afterwards I heard challenging shouts from the sentries and a few shots rang out.

Before long the firing ceased. That might mean either that the guerrillas intended to leave me in peace to my fate or that they would organise a party to go in search of me at daybreak, as they obviously could not do such a thing at night.

Next day there seemed to be no sign of any pursuit. But I now found myself in a dilemma. On the one hand it would be better not to seek out anyone in case the person I met should prove to be hostile and on the other hand it was absolutely necessary to find someone in order to ask the way.

I remained in the first of these cases for the time being. Time went on and on and I saw no one. The horses were showing a lot of nervousness after their recent experiences. Young Luchador whinnied plaintively almost continuously in his fear of wild beasts, and kept kicking out; I could hardly control him.

After dismounting, while I was leading the animal, I made a false step over some fallen leaves that concealed a deep hole full of muddy water. I sank into it up to the breast and felt myself continuing to sink. In a panic I gripped the bridle reins hard. It seemed as though Young Luchador understood what he had to do. He backed slowly, with his neck stretched well out, tugging me out of the semi-liquid mud, and I was gradually pulled clear of it. As soon as I had climbed back on hands and knees into the undergrowth I uttered an immense sigh of relief; it had been a fairly close thing.

Meanwhile something much more serious had occurred in relation to the other horse. Fury had bolted or at any rate disappeared during the incident and though I called him at the top of my voice I could not hear a single answering neigh. Mounting Young Luchador, I made up my mind to search that appalling wilderness in every direction. But I had very little hope of finding the horse I had lost. I noticed that Young Luchador seemed reluctant to obey me. He preferred, apparently, to follow his own devices. I realised then that it would be better to allow him to do so. I let the reins lie loose, to give him his head, and he soon led me to a spot where Fury was standing, hemmed in on all sides by huge bushes.

At that point the summits of the trees grew so close together that they completely veiled the sky and the sunlight, just at the time when I had particular need of the sun's rays to dry my caked and dripping garments.

I finally discovered a place where a little light came through, the leaves of the trees round about being withered. I stayed there till I and my clothes were dry.

Then the worst happened; I could see a number of paths or tracks which appeared to serve as such but I could not decide which of them led in the right direction. While I was still busy with this problem of orientation the day waned and night found me not yet sure of the way. I determined to call a halt and try to sleep a little. But sleep evaded me. At night the forest seemed more menacing than ever. The air was full of sounds which suggested the ceaseless commotion of millions of tiny creatures. From time to time sinister howlings, piercing outcries that might have come from miles away or only a distance of a yard or two, could be heard. In the intervening silences, haunted by vague murmurs to which our ears grew more and more sensitive, we fancied we could distinguish the hissing breath of feline beasts of prey, the patient gnawing of rodents, the gliding of cold and slimy reptiles and the restless activity of innumerable insects. In any case, quite apart from such sensations as these, the hordes of mosquitoes would have prevented me from sleeping.

Accordingly, I resumed my journey and was traversing a path which I needed the utmost concentration of all my five senses not to lose when, just before midnight, I came upon a few huts occupied by negroes. They received me hospitably and offered me what they could from their slender resources. I obtained a little unhusked rice for the horses and for myself the indispensable loan of a mosquito-net, which enabled me at last to enjoy the sleep of which I had so long been deprived.

In the morning the blacks told me that I was in the heart of the country of the bandits or guerrillas, and actually, when I renewed my travels that day, following the somewhat indefinite directions given me by the negroes, I found at various times two or three more camps of refugees in the woods.

It was not always easy to recognise which side these parties belonged to. I could only guess that when they all wore more or less the same uniform they were probably Government troops.

Sometimes a man from one faction or the other would escort me as far as the next camp. But after a while I had no more such luck and had to go on alone, trying continually to fix in my memory the details of the information given me as to the correct route. I was constantly obliged to change direction in order to avoid rivers, watercourses, impassable tracks and several zones of thick black mud and marshland.

In one of these the horses got bogged down. The harder I worked to bring them out of it the deeper they sank. At last only their heads, necks and part of their backs showed above the mud and I began to think I was going to lose them for ever. I rushed off to the camp I had just left, ignoring the lacerations inflicted on my flesh and clothing by the thorns of the undergrowth, and pleaded for help. The men from the camp returned with me to the spot bringing ropes with them. By fastening these to the animals we succeeded in the end, after terrific efforts, in hoisting the horses out of the bog. They had nearly been buried alive.

Exhausted as I was by all these misfortunes, I lost myself completely, during the next stage of the ride, in the mazes of the jungle. It is infuriating not to know which point of the compass one is facing. One no sooner decides to take certain kinds of trees or bushes as landmarks than they turn up in all directions at once. On the other hand if, with the intention of avoiding all possibility of error, you undertake brief scouting expeditions, you find that every twenty yards you cover means a fierce struggle with the obstacles presented by the forest, its whipping branches, its banks of fallen leaves and the tripping roots and pitfalls in the ground.

I had been told at the last camp I visited that the Government intended to send out a military search-party for me unless it heard during the next few days where I was or that I had already reached the places scheduled on my route.

For this reason I could not be sure, when I heard shots, whether they were fired by the soldiers who were looking for me with the object of indicating where I could find them or whether one of those skirmishes or pitched battles between the two factions of the civil war was going on.

The firing died down at last and I remained for all practical purposes lost in the jungle, with its terrible masses of greenery pressing in upon me from all sides. A time came when I could go no further, even for a couple of yards, without first tearing down that formidable barrier. For some time I busied myself with this task, bare-handed, till my whole body was furrowed and bleeding from the wounds inflicted by thorns and branches.

From a hut on some open ground where there had once, apparently, been water, three men came out to meet me. Knowing as I did the political situation, I had no desire to ask who they were, what they were doing there or even which side they were on. I succeeded in inducing one of them to come with me and open up a way through the tangle of vegetation with his sharp and heavy *machete*. I asked him to lend me another so that I could help him. I was much slower at the work and admired the dexterity with which he rapidly cleared a passage through the shrubs and bushes that had to be cut away.

But after some hours of this gruelling toil it began to grow dark. The man ceased his labours and announced:

"I'm going back to the hut now. I can't do any more. You'd better come with me."

I did not want to do this as it would have meant going back on my hard-won advance and so I was once more alone, with the dreadful jungle night about me; I remember that I spent those hours of impenetrable darkness in one of those fits of loneliness and depression that occasionally overcame me, till I felt I should never be able to continue. I wept bitterly, bathing the muzzles of the horses with my tears. The screams and howls of the nocturnal forest filled me with terror.

I gradually managed to overcome my fits of panic. I spent two months altogether in that jungle, lost and alone for more than two-thirds of the time. On certain days I was reduced to such extremities by solitude and hardship that I found myself forced by hunger to eat the very flowers that grew so plentifully in the forest. I had asked some boys at a ranch which of the flowers were the least poisonous. Though the information they gave me was somewhat vague, hunger resolved all my doubts and scruples. The flowers not only provided me with a meal on the few occasions when I was obliged to eat them. They also furnished me sometimes with an enchanting spectacle. I was fascinated in particular by the orchids, with their numerous intricate shapes and shades of colour, as they climbed towards the source of light up the soaring branches of the trees.

With such training in the lore of the jungle I began to grow accustomed to the events, great and small, which

With Mexican Indians.

With policemen in Texas.

Crossing a town in Alabama, U.S.A., in the rain.

Arrival at the Argentine Embassy in Ottawa.

characterise life in the woods and with which I was to become even more familiar in the forests of Central America that lay before me. For example, the first time one of the spiders called *pollitos* (chickens) dropped on my knees while I was lying on the ground, still half asleep after a night's rest, I jumped up and screamed, though no one but my horses could have heard me. The insect was as big as a crab or a large toad and its hairy legs made me shudder with disgust. The creature gave me an awful fright. But as later on I came across such spiders fairly frequently I gradually lost all fear of them and nearly all the repugnance I felt at their appearance, till in the end I quite enjoyed studying the diversity of their colouring.

My only objection to them was that their bite might injure the horses. I took preventive measures against such bites and also against those of other kinds of dangerous vermin by rubbing the lower parts of the horses' legs with garlic, the smell of which, I had been told, repels spiders, small vipers and other horrid creatures of that sort.

My pilgrimage through the woods came to an end at Turbo on the Gulf of Uraba, in north-west Colombia.

Chapter XIII

STORM AND PIRATES

At this stage I was confronted by a problem that directly concerned my ride and my integrity as a sportswoman. It was not possible to leave Colombia for Panama, the next republic on my route, without crossing the waters of the gulf. The northern coast of Colombia ends at this gulf and beyond it lies the great Caribbean.

I racked my brains to think of some way of avoiding interruption of the continuity of the ride by land. I even thought at one time of returning to Medellin and setting out due north from that city to Barranquilla, further to the east along the coast. Or again I might ride back along the shores of the gulf to Cartagena.

As though all these worries were not enough, I began to suffer incessant pain in my back teeth. This detail may not be regarded as a major setback on such a journey as mine but I could not put it out of my mind. Chance brought me in contact, at a small farm, with a doctor. I could not find a dentist nor any instrument with which to rid myself of the trouble. The only tool the doctor could offer me was a pair of ordinary pincers. I delivered myself up into his hands and whatever strength they might be able to exert.

Minus one of my back teeth and still in great pain I took the only decision open to me in the circumstances: it was absolutely impossible to continue by land. In Turbo I had the opportunity of hiring a motor-driven craft normally employed in the banana trade, plying across the Gulf of Uraba. She was called the *Santa Lucia*. The first serious trouble started as soon as we tried to embark the horses, though the entire population of a coastal village lent their aid. We used a crane, but it did not look as if the operation would ever succeed. Several times the animals fell into the water and I was left in agonies of worry, almost wishing I had never suggested such a method of embarkation. Three hours passed before the heroic Young Luchador and Fury were safely installed aboard the vessel, a cargo boat of some 150 tons, manned by a crew whose faces were not very reassuring, their gestures wild and their movements and behaviour quite undisciplined. A personage of the name of Ulysses acted as skipper. I gathered from the arguments and discussions of the crew that they were at sea as freelances or pirates, having got rid of their legitimate captain by some violent means or other—I guessed he was a Conservative—and that they had no fixed plans, except that they were most anxious not to fall into the hands of any representatives of the Government.

Perhaps I ought not to have taken the risk of going aboard a vessel I knew nothing about, but I did not have very much choice, owing to the low state of my finances. My recent expenses had accounted for the last of my slender resources and I was now utterly penniless.

To make matters worse we ran into a storm in the Gulf. The little craft rolled dangerously from side to side, the waves dashed furiously against her sides and covered the deck with a perpetually swirling mass of foam. The wind rose to hurricane strength, battering at our temples and ears. Everyone was bawling at everyone else. The horses continually slipped and bruised themselves badly as the vessel rolled.

I overheard fragments of the talk of some of the crew as the horses went staggering about the deck and realised that they were hatching the worst of plots. The weight of the animals was endangering the safety of the vessel as she laboured in the storm and they were thinking of lightening her by throwing the poor beasts overboard.

I reprimanded them at the top of my voice, trying to make my protests heard above the howling of the wind. The horses also neighed piteously, as though they were human beings in mortal danger. The battering of the waves against the

sides of the ship threatened to smash them in at any moment.
From time to time flashes of forked lightning illumined the
scene and I could see my horses rearing and lashing out in all
directions, maddened with terror, and flung heavily in all
directions. They were screaming shrilly, like souls in torment.

My shouts of indignation had steadied the attitude of the
crew to some extent. I wanted to lay my grievances before
the man who was acting as captain. But he had locked himself
in his cabin, pretending to be ill, and would not listen to
anybody.

I remember catching sight of a little old woman—heaven
only knows what she was doing aboard—drenched to the
skin and sheltering from the storm as well as she could, who
still had enough strength left to call out to me:

"Look after yourself and don't worry about the horses!"

The ancient creature was so astonished at my behaviour that
I saw her, in the light of one of the flashes, cross herself, and
heard her mutter:

"Holy Mary, I wouldn't risk my life for those brutes even
if they were Christians!"

I realised that the amateur crew had completely lost their
bearings. One of them, who was a negro, swarmed up the
topmast, which was swaying wildly in the hurricane. I
gathered from his gestures that he had sighted a bay in which
we might take refuge and cast anchor, which we eventually
did, halfway on our course.

The storm died down and soon afterwards we made
Cartagena, where the crew got into quite serious trouble
with the authorities. I myself, as soon as I had explained who
I was, received very different treatment.

But I found myself obliged to remain in the port for about
four months, involved in the usual discussions and formalities
which almost invariably ensue when there is any question of
crossing a frontier. On this occasion the matter was com-
plicated by my lack of funds. Nevertheless, it was essential
for me to obtain a passage. It was only because it turned out
to be physically impossible for any human being to reach
Panama by land, along the shores of the gulf, that I consented

to go by sea. I feel I ought not to omit this point, as this was the sole occasion throughout my ride that I covered even a brief stage of the journey by water, with my horses aboard.

I shall always remember Cartagena as a precious relic of the ancient American tradition. The oldest part of the city, its most truly typical buildings, are surrounded by mighty ramparts constructed by the Spaniards. They enabled the place to withstand sieges by buccaneers and English armies and to repel all attempts at invasion.

The territory already referred to, which I had decided not to try to cross, consisted of wild, impenetrable country, with endless marshes, flooded regions and inaccessible mountains. It formed a barrier which I could never have passed alone and still less with the horses. Though my decision to embark was forced upon me quite inevitably, I should like to record the events of this short interval in my journey by land just as they happened.

On the purely financial side, I was told that the regular fare by sea from Cartagena to Colón amounted to 500 dollars, representing an astronomical figure for me at that period. I could no more have paid such a sum than I could have bought all the estates in the province of Buenos Aires.

I argued, by way of advancing security, that the Argentine Government had recommended that I should be given every facility and that the special character of the journey I had planned should be taken into consideration. But these observations had no effect. I was met with a blank wall of refusal.

I returned to Medellin by air, so that the horses could be given a rest, as they had travelled all the stages of the ride hitherto. I was doing no more, on this occasion, than using the means of transport which may be regarded as the most popular in these big South American countries, with their long stretches of woods and mountains. The Indians themselves are in the habit of travelling by air, sometimes taking their goods and chattels with them, including occasionally their chickens. I explained matters in the first place to the Riding Club. The members generously assisted me to meet the expenses of pressing on with my plan in these altered conditions. The most active of them in giving such assistance practical expression was Señora Luz de Gutierrez. I should emphasise that aid of this kind was always limited to what was absolutely necessary to enable me to move on and only when exceptional circumstances required it.

On my return to Cartagena I found that the jungle of obstacles confronting me, though I was not now travelling on horseback through one, rivalled the entanglements of the physical jungle itself. I was told on all sides that I should not be allowed to land in Panama in any case on account of foot-and-mouth disease. "My horses have never had foot-and-mouth disease," I answered, but regulations, it seemed, were regulations.

Accordingly, I decided to try my luck at the North American Naval Mission, where I was informed that my case would be referred to the authorities at Colón. From Colón I received a reply which promised that I should be granted all possible facilities. In order to discover what such facilities might be and whether they would prove of real advantage to me I took a passage on a small cargo steamer to that city. The accommodation aboard was very cramped, especially that for the horses. They had to stand on slippery iron plates and suffered as they always did on any voyage. It was no wonder that whenever they saw ships or boats they directed passionately imploring glances at me as if begging that we might always stay on dry land.

Apart from the brief sea-voyage that I made, Colombia, in all its beauty, variety and exuberance, had been the scene of many of my most exciting adventures. Despite the civil war that was raging at the time of my journey through many of its districts I was almost always helped by the men I met in different parts of the country, including the negroes and half-breeds as well as the Indians.

Our voyage to Colón involved a great many disputes and complex operations concerned with the embarkation of the horses. At first no one would take them aboard and subsequently the smallest craft demanded 600 dollars for doing so.

Eventually we landed on Panamanian soil, in the United States zone. As I only possessed Colombian currency the official requirements that had to be met before the horses could be put ashore proved more troublesome than ever and in fact almost insurmountable.

The next stage was to ride through the territory of Panama as I had ridden through that of the other republics. During the early part of the journey I had the good fortune to be entertained at the house of a certain Don Roberto, a planter, whose hospitality I shall never forget. I had been worn out by a long ride over rugged mountain country, much of it covered with forest, and was obliged to stay in bed at his place for a few days, trying to cure my gastritis by drinking a glass of sour milk every morning and taking no other food.

When I took to the road again I found the going as rough and mountainous as ever. My three days without food had deprived me of much of my strength. In this condition I arrived at a small inn kept by a swarthy half-breed who gave my horses and myself all we needed without charging me anything.

At a slightly later stage in the journey I was unable to find any place at which my horses could receive the attention they so urgently required. The occupants of a hut close by told me that 'away up there, very high up', at the very summit of the mountain, lived a certain 'Señor Pol', who was highly regarded in all the plantations and families of the neighbourhood. My informants added: "And how long do you think it will take you to get there with those animals of yours?" As on so many previous occasions, I made no reply to this question, privately reflecting, 'That's my business.'

To describe our ascent to the peak would merely be to repeat former narratives of such wearisome climbs, already recounted in these pages. When we reached the top a man of good-natured and rustic appearance, dressed with rural simplicity, accosted us.

"I am looking for Señor Pol," I said. "Could you tell me where to find his house?"

"I think so," he answered, laughing heartily. "I'm the man you're looking for."

Both I and my two faithful companions received every attention, and Señor Pol, in his generosity, hit upon the notion of organising a lottery among his local acquaintances, in order to raise enough money to pay my expenses as far as the city of Panama.

I remained in that capital for eight days and everyone I met was most kind to me. Press and radio spread the news of my arrival and were lavish in their praises of this and that aspect of my adventures. I was really treated like a heroine. When I made a public appearance with my horses at the Riding School, the place was crammed with cheering spectators. One does not have to be very conceited to find a certain compensation in such moments, in the affectionate and loyal tributes of good-natured people, as well as renewed courage in the recognition that such occasions cancel out the misery and hardship endured during other stages of the trip.

I crossed the famous canal that divides the continent of America in two, riding over the New Bridge and reflecting that the canal also divided my ride into two separate sections. When I passed through the towns of Chorrera and Penomone, in the Rio Grande district, I was delighted to see the local schoolchildren drawn up to welcome me and cheering the Republic of Argentina. Another event by which I was deeply moved and which compensated me for my labours in the way mentioned above was my reception by Dr. Arias, President of Panama, and his wife, Señora Ana Linares de Arias. They invited me to a most enjoyable breakfast party, which I shall always remember. It was given at their estate and coffee plantation of El Boquete. Among the courtesies they offered me was one of an economic nature, which enabled me to relieve my chronic shortage of currency a little.

But soon afterwards, just to remind me that my routine was not to vary, I plunged once more into the woods, and forgetfulness of congratulations and entertainments.

At a place called Cañas Gordas, at the frontier of Costa Rica, on the road from Concepción, I had to cross the Old

Chiriqui river by an extremely dangerous pontoon which swayed in the current like a paper boat. The only way to do it was to lead first one horse and then the other. Beyond Cañas Gordas stretches a thickly wooded and mountainous tract called by the local people 'Come out if you can'. One of the natives of the place told me that the devil himself, if he tried it with a couple of horses like mine, would never be able to get through that bit of country. Not everyone was quite so positive about it as this, but the great majority were unanimously of the opinion that to cross that region would be practically impossible.

It consisted of a long defile walled in on both sides by rocks and masses of tangled vegetation. I saw at once that though it might well prove impossible to 'come out', as the local phrase had it, it was quite certain that once one was in one could not turn back. As soon as the horses had entered the gorge and begun slowly to make their way along it, they were physically incapable of retracing their steps. Incessant streams of water ran over the level bottom along which we were bound to proceed. The agitated snorting of the animals aroused my heartfelt sympathy. But I had to keep them steadily on the move if we were to find our way out of that dreaded 'Come out if you can.'

On this occasion we managed it. I entered Costa Rica without any trouble over papers and passports, for this was a region shunned as much by Customs officials as indeed by almost all other civilised people.

I met no one on the road, which was deep in mud of various colours; the horses sank into it up to their bellies.

The new Pan-American highway had been scheduled to begin at Cañas Gordas. But at the time I was travelling through this part of the country it had only reached the planning stage. Consequently, I had once more to plunge into the jungle and even to revise my previous opinion that the Colombian section would prove to be the most difficult stage of the journey. The Colombian jungle at any rate had been frequented by roving bands of guerrillas, undisciplined and dangerous to travellers as they might be: but on the Costa Rica side it did not even seem that anybody at all had any desire to seclude themselves within its shelter. Moreover, all the characteristic jungle obstacles of impenetrable vegetation and sudden steep inclines had to be reckoned with once more.

Though there were no human beings, the region was alive with birds of every hue, insects of every imaginable shape and swarms of animals bustling about in the thickets. A great variety of reptiles, of all the colours of the rainbow, was also to be seen crossing our path; of some we only caught a brief glimpse, but the presence of vipers was invariably registered by the horses kicking out.

Nevertheless, all this would have been tolerable enough if it had not been for the accident which befell Fury at one of the steepest precipices we came across. I was feeling exhausted at the time, after having had to cut a long path for the horses through the tangled undergrowth. I had never realised how bulky an animal a horse is till I found that mine were held up wherever the path narrowed. I had also been obliged to drag away fallen tree-trunks that were blocking the road, though only those, of course, which were small enough for my limited physical powers to cope with. The big ones formed regular barriers which we had to surmount as best we could by climbing over them. I reached a point when I could no longer hold the *machete*, the muscles of my arms being utterly worn out by cutting brushwood. We were struggling up an almost vertical incline when Fury slipped and fell right to the bottom of the cliff. I uttered a shrill scream, which was echoed by a number of birds of the parrot type from the tops of the surrounding trees. I was at a loss to know what to do next. It was essential for me to keep my footing on the incline and also at the same time to make sure that Young Luchador did not in his turn lose his balance and roll to the bottom.

Fury being down below, in what condition I had no idea, and his companion at my side, the two of us spent the night standing up, as neither the horse nor myself could lie down. Everyone knows how many hours there are in a night. But no one can have the slightest notion how long such a night as that takes to pass. I thought daybreak would never come. The intensity of the weariness in my limbs equalled that of the dread in my heart. I believed every sound I heard came from some huge snake or terrible beast of prey about to attack me. What could they not do to a horse away down there, far out of my sight?

As dawn broke I saw three men approaching. I knew at once that they were smugglers, for by this time I had learnt, at the frontiers, what they looked like. They were walking very fast, as their business required, and showed no inclination whatever to stop.

I called out to them, begging them to help me extricate Fury from wherever he had fallen. They replied that the place was too far down and that they had no time to undertake so difficult a task.

I offered to give them, as a reward for the work, the splendid rifle presented to me by the Panamanian Chief of Police. Its loss would leave me badly off for weapons, since I should then only have my revolver. But my horse was well worth all the rifles in the world, even taking into consideration the services that particular rifle had rendered me. I had often used it to bring down good-sized birds, which I plucked without troubling myself how beautiful their plumage might be and roasted over an improvised fire, on a spit. The methods I employed, during my ride, for 'living off the country' were many and various.

The men accepted my offer. For two hours they worked at clearing paths up the cliff by which Fury could ascend without much difficulty. But it was some time before the horse would move and I began to be afraid my helpers would grow tired of trying to make him. At last he showed signs of life and the men managed to bring him up; the three of us were together again.

Two or three miles further on I came, to my relief, upon a small log-cabin, where I took refuge while the animals regained their strength by grazing on such pasture as they could find. I removed my boots, which were dripping wet and plastered thick with mud, and put them to dry by a fire of logs which I kindled. The result of this rash proceeding was that their nails came out. Accordingly, I was now left without boots.

That night my feet swelled, keeping me awake, as did also the creeping of the most various kinds of animals over me. They included dogs, rats, and even, I believe, toads.

With or without boots, I had to continue my journey. I put on slippers, though I might just as well have gone barefoot for all the use they were in that frightful mud; I did not keep them on long.

Some sixty miles from Concepción I crossed a bridge only negotiable by horses if they went in single file and walked as on a tightrope. I was then confronted by the famous La Pita mountain, famous for its almost inaccessible character. Nor shall I forget its reputation in a hurry; I shall always remember that painful climb, barefooted as I was, on the razor-edged rocks, for it proved quite impossible to ride. I had more than enough to do in making sure that the animals at least did not lose their footing. Even so, Young Luchador was flung back on his haunches and began to slide down several times.

I had lost my slippers, having thrown them away, and when I reached the top of the mountain I lost consciousness as well, for a while, owing to the altitude.

CHAPTER XIV

BAREFOOT AMONG THE VIPERS

I now found myself among the soaring peaks of the Talamanca range; the going was extremely difficult. I had noticed quite a number of people at work on the mountain slopes and their operations rather intrigued me; they came from San José, the capital of the country, and were engaged in company with some aboriginal inhabitants of the zone on excavation work, sometimes digging up ancient relics in the form of fragments of pottery, figurines and, not infrequently, gold. The lion's share of these finds, if the discoveries were made by the aboriginals, went to the local headman. Otherwise such objects remained the property of those who found them.

As I had nothing better to do while the animals were resting, I borrowed a pickaxe and spent the whole day digging in the hope that I, too, might find some gold. On certain days, I was told, prodigious discoveries were made. Genuine auriferous seams turned up, compensating those lucky enough to find them with magnificent rewards for their pains. So far as I myself was concerned, I got nothing but corns and blisters all over my hands.

An Indian woman told me that her mother had once found quite a lot of gold, nearly as much as she could carry in her joined palms. It was true that her mother had never found anything before or since and that it all happened very long ago and it must be admitted that her discovery didn't do her the slightest good as the gold was stolen from her on the way home by persons unknown, or at any rate unknown to their victim.

There were many wild boars in the district, the heavily

timbered and mountainous environment favouring their survival. Consequently the staple food of the region consisted of their meat, cooked with a little rice. The dish sounds appetising enough to suit anyone occasionally but when served every day without exception it inevitably becomes dreary fare and ends by being monotonous.

I took part with much enthusiasm in the boar hunts and was only sorry that I had given away that excellent rifle of mine to the smugglers as a reward for their assistance. Decent firearms were scarce among the hunters but a half-breed lent me his shot-gun, which was not at all a bad weapon, and I was able to boast of my marksmanship after wounding a boar which was later despatched some two miles further on. The sport was not dangerous if one refrained from trying to stop an escaping animal on a narrow path. All the same, two of the hunters I accompanied had been lamed by boars' tusks.

I was obliged to join the aboriginals in drinking their fermented liquor, made from sugar-cane. It is officially prohibited but nevertheless often drunk. If not taken to excess it gives renewed strength to persons who, like myself, have gone through a good deal of strain.

After this I had to cross a very wide river—I think it was the Brus—in a canoe, while the horses swam alongside. The strong current persistently carried the animals away and I had my work cut out to counteract it. Fury in particular gave me a lot to do, being more nervous and timid than the other horse. For that reason, whenever we came to a dangerous place on the route I always rode Young Luchador and kept hold of Fury's bridle-rein.

I was on this stage of the journey when I was terrified to see an enormous serpent glide, with undulating movements, across the path a few yards ahead. The creature was as thick as the calf of my leg. I couldn't give its length, for it seemed to me in my fright to take half an hour to cross the path. The horses shook all over and so did I. But fortunately on that occasion nothing happened but the slow unfolding of the brilliant colours of the slimy body of the reptile, as it slid along without taking any notice of us.

A little further on we saw another great viper. This one, which was coiled round the branch of a tree, merely moved its delicately shaped head a little as we approached. I now believe that it did so because it had seen us and was wondering what it should do next, though of course the movement might have been a purely casual one. In any case we left the path when we caught sight of the creature and, at the cost of a number of long, deep scratches and thorn-pricks, gave the snake in the tree as wide a berth as possible.

In a small clearing we came upon an encampment occupied by natives. A few young girls appeared as we approached but, after watching us intently for a few moments, took to flight. The other Indians who then showed themselves behaved in the same manner.

I called out to them at the top of my voice: "Give me some water!"

After some hesitation they went to fetch water and brought it to me. After placing it on the ground they again retreated rapidly.

"I want something to eat!" I shouted, as loudly as before.

"We've got nothing, nothing at all," they answered.

"What about those bananas over there?"

I had mentioned the bananas as they appeared to be the only eatable things in sight. The Indians brought me a few, though as timidly as before.

When my companions and I had eaten and drunk our fill of the bananas and the water, our temporary satisfaction evaporated on finding that all the paths leading out of the clearing appeared to have been completely planted over.

It was no good going on unless I could find someone from whom I could ask the way. The Indian women in the camp we had just left had not replied to the questions I had put to them in this connection.

As luck would have it, we met two women carrying bundles of sugar-cane on their heads. The horses made quite a rush at them in order to help themselves to the cane. This incident and the strangeness of my appearance in that part of the country, where they had never seen anything like me before, surprised and frightened the women. But I was able to reassure them to a certain extent by explaining the reasons for my presence.

One of the women, who had a child with her, escorted me to some other huts belonging to Indians, where she had the hospitable idea of begging a meal for me. I was promptly served with a dish containing bird's meat, which seemed to show that they were unexpectedly well off for food. After I had eaten the entire contents of the dish, though I found them on the tough side, I enquired what sort of a bird it was.

"It's just a bird," they answered.

"But what kind of bird? What colour is it?"

"Green. Very bright. Very pretty."

They showed me its head, which had a curved beak. I had eaten a parrot!

I was fairly well used to atrocious food by that time and ate almost anything that came along. But that parrot turned my stomach. I felt ill for some days after it.

The woman who had served me with this meal had a son, a young fellow about twenty, whom she requested to escort me on my way for a few days. "If you go with this young woman," his mother instructed him, "God will reward you."

The prospect of this benefit induced him to obey, though in somewhat faint-hearted a fashion, for despite his familiarity with life in the forest he seemed to be in considerable fear of the vipers and other predatory creatures. He insisted on my going ahead of him and I soon got tired of this method of progress, for I, too, dreaded the job of clearing a way through the jungle.

The Indian worked with a *machete*, his chief task being to cut a path, however narrow, for the horses. But whenever there were any serious obstructions and the work of removing them proved at all hard, he invariably told me:

"The big animal doesn't want to go that way."

It was not so much the fact that the horse didn't want to go in that direction, but that he simply couldn't, which only showed with what reluctance the young man continued to wield his *machete*.

144

He went with me as far as the river Brujo ('Wizard'). The name was most appropriate, though it was less the stream than the person who crossed it that should have been called a wizard. The river was a torrential medley of stones and water which we forded, with our hearts in our mouths, by a series of miracles. The water-plants grew so densely that they wound themselves round my body, dragging me out of the saddle when the horse got clear of them.

I came at last to a small village where I decided to rest for a few days. All three of us were now so weak that we could not summon up enough strength to go on. The place was full of oranges and we spent quite a lot of time consuming this appetising fruit, which appeases both hunger and thirst simultaneously.

My two horses were in a sad state by this time. They had been without shoes ever since leaving Concepción and Fury was suffering from a hoof-distemper which had much enfeebled him.

Later on, following an almost invisible track, I arrived at a small town called Buenos Aires, which, however, recalled the distant and opulent capital of my native land in name only. There I found a North American blacksmith who shod my horses. The shoes came off, subsequently, during our long rides over rocks and flooded territory, which softened the hoofs of the animals, causing the nails to loosen and drop out.

After leaving Buenos Aires I found myself on more even ground. It was a great relief not to have to contend with slopes up or down hill as well as the obstructions of the thickets.

I saw a snake which appeared to me to be of gigantic size— I suppose it really did measure some nine feet—devouring a small animal which, so far as I could see, looked like an uncommonly big hare. The same day I saw another snake, but a smaller one, swallowing a toad of which only the yellowish green legs still remained visible. The sight reminded me of an occasion in Colombia, near Ibague, when a toad had persistently followed me for a considerable distance. I had slowed down out of curiosity, wondering what could be the reason for such a dogged pursuit. Then I remembered having heard that these reptiles when pursued by a viper often follow a human being in order to escape attack by the snake. Up to that time I had not been able to ascertain whether the story was a mere fable or had some truth in it; I was now furnished with proof, for at a discreet distance, well away from the path, I could see the viper gliding along after its coveted prey. The conscientious anxiety with which the poor toad was scampering as fast as its feeble legs could carry it, with its gaze fixed on the horses' legs, was perfectly obvious.

I had always been informed that the dangerous vipers are not as a rule those of large dimensions, unless one trod on them by accident, causing them to fear an attack at close quarters. The really dangerous ones, with virulently poisonous bites, are seldom of any great length. However, an Indian whom I met and talked with for a time on that same path told me that I should find, about a mile further on, the skeleton of a mule lying beside the track; the beast had belonged to some people who were travelling from Buenos Aires to San Isidro. It had strayed, he said, and been strangled in the coils of one of the bigger snakes. I thought myself it might have received a fatal bite from some poisonous variety, as occurs very often in all the forests of Central America, the victims being as frequently human beings as animals. I remember in this connection that I once saw, in Panama, the corpse of a little Indian girl shortly after she had died as the result of being bitten by a small snake. I have now forgotten the local name given to the reptile in question, but it was the same as that of the huge serpent mentioned by the Indian I met on the track going to Potrero Grande, the snake which he said had killed the mule.

While we are on the subject of these reptiles, which swarm in the woods of this part of America, I may add that the only serpent I ever contemplated, during my ride, with complete equanimity, so as to be able to make a minute examination of it, was a rattlesnake. It was a splendid specimen of the breed and had been killed by some Indian foresters. They had intended to play a trick on me by disposing the dead creature in natural coils, so as to frighten me out of my wits before I noticed that it did not move. As soon as I found the reptile was not alive I inspected it carefully.

I found that the tail ended in a singular appendage, which is the source of the well-known shrill rattle; it had fourteen closely fitting rings. The head was small and the body was covered with compact scales, maroon and reddish yellow in colour, with several rows of bright yellow dots that formed regular designs. I was told that the poison is extremely virulent, being concentrated in a depression of the long, curved teeth, by means of which the bite is inflicted and the poison discharged. The venom acts directly on the nervous system and is the cause of many deaths. They shed their skins two or three times a year. When I asked whether the rings of the rattle were good for anything, one of the men told me that warning of the snake's approach was by this means given to other animals and to human beings. He cited this explanation as a proof of the wisdom of Nature, the rattler's venom being so deadly. But another contradicted him, saying that the sound served to attract the reptiles to one another at the breeding season. This view I should think the most likely of the two.

It was while I was here that I tried my hand at gold-mining. A large number of Indians were excavating galleries of great depth, which passed beneath tombs of great antiquity, where persons of note, according to local belief, had been buried. As on the previous occasion, I took advantage of this opportunity to rest the animals while I dug strenuously, in a state of profuse perspiration, for two days. In spite of the repeated statements of an optimistic nature made by the amateur miners, I obtained merely handfuls of bruises and blisters for my trouble, with never a glimpse of the gold alleged to be stored in the tombs.

I was obliged to remain in San Isidro del General for several days, as Fury's hoof-distemper still needed rest. At this place construction of certain stages of the Pan-American highway had already started.

On leaving the town I was most anxious to reach Cartago, where I had reason to hope that conditions would be considerably easier. I had to undergo first the fatigue of climbing the mountain locally known as the Peak of Death. As if this exhausting labour were not enough in itself, night surprised me at the foot of the peak itself, chilling me to the bone.

By way of compensation I was accorded a magnificent reception in Cartago, which I badly needed, for I felt wretched and looked worse. Don Carlos Fernandez, the Argentine ambassador, who had come from San José to welcome me, and the Labour leader, Señor Arturo Sacomani, were waiting for me. Both greeted me with the utmost affability and cordiality but they could not get over their astonishment at the shabbiness of my clothing.

"How do you feel?" Sacomani asked.

"As you see—a bit done in."

"But how is it going, really?" he repeated.

"It's going barefooted," I retorted, with a grin.

It was a fact that the mud and the stones had ruined my slippers and I had nothing to put on my feet.

Later on we left for San José, the capital of Costa Rica, where Sacomani presented me with a costume such as the *gauchos* on his estate wore. It suited me in every sense of the word. It fitted me excellently and at the same time supplied the deficiency of my wardrobe for the rest of the ride.

Both Press and radio had announced the place at which I would enter the city and I was ambushed by a horde of little boys, who cheered me to the echo. The noise they made was so strident that I feared at first it might indicate hostility or jeers at my shabby appearance. But my companions soon reassured me. The boys, they said, were simply showing their delight at my arrival.

On the first Sunday of my stay at San José the famous Racing Argentine polo team played the local club. I rode round the field, which was decorated with the flags of Costa Rica and Argentina, and received a positive ovation from the crowd as I passed with my horses.

My grateful recollections of the pleasant days I spent in San José have almost made me forget to record a terrific kick in the face which my dear companion Young Luchador treated me to near Puntarenas. I had been playing with him, as I often did, trying to make him lift his foreleg or hoof according to the directions I gave him. As he obstinately declined to obey me, I rebuked him in good old Creole fashion.

"You won't, eh? All right, then, go to the devil!"

I gave him a light flick across the muzzle and then, before I could turn my back on him, he kicked me in the face and bolted.

Fortunately, I had stepped back like lightning, so that the impact of the iron shoe did not strike me with all its force. All the same, the blow was hard enough to knock me right out. When I came to myself I found I had a great bruise on the cheek and a loosened back-tooth.

I spent New Year's Day in a village near Puntarenas, where rice was being milled. I therefore had a good opportunity here to feed my two animals, who were, as usual, ravenous.

At Liberia I noticed that preparatory work on the Pan-American highway was going on, though no part of the surface had yet been laid. In the La Cruz and Peña Blanca regions, adjoining the Nicaraguan frontier, there were no roads at all. I was obliged once more to undergo the experiences of the worst days of my journey, clambering across mountainous territory with fearfully precipitous ascents and descents; both horses and rider had to struggle ceaselessly to maintain balance.

The most remarkable sight I saw that first day was a closely coiled viper 'sitting' on its eggs in a nest of dry straw. Apparently this was the open season for reptiles. Next day I found that another viper, of an emerald green colour, had coiled itself round one of Fury's legs. The horse nearly went mad with fright, finally succeeding, by some trick I can't imagine, in getting rid of the snake by a violent shake of his foreleg as he reared and caracoled in his panic.

I had no sooner entered Nicaraguan territory when I was struck with admiration at the sight of the proud, majestic splendour of the volcanic heights. Here I was suddenly taken so ill that I could not dream of pressing on to Managua, as I had intended. The symptoms began to show themselves at Belen. I had to stop while riding through a coffee plantation and it was there that I was found later, unconscious. I had been riding ever since dawn under a merciless sun. The planter's family were most prompt in coming to my rescue. They informed the Argentine Embassy of my plight and the Briceno family took me to San Marcos.

As nearly always happened, I soon recovered after a short rest and rode on to Managua where I was most hospitably received. I took the opportunity of an interview with President Somoza to make a request for something of which I stood desperately in need. My forest wanderings and the long distances traversed between inhabited places had shown me the necessity of providing myself with a weapon in better condition than my revolver. I wanted one of fairly large calibre, quite new, which would be efficient and reliable in any sudden emergency. The President was very nice about it and gaily agreed to supply such a weapon. But, despite my repeated reminders, the promise he had made always seemed to slip his memory. I could well understand that it would be difficult for such a busy man to remember such a trifle, but tenacity is one of my few virtues; I went and sat under a tree on his country estate, the Monte Linares plantation. Soon I caught sight of the lorry filled with machine-gunners that heralded the approach of the General's car. When it drove up to the house and he alighted, I emerged from my hiding-place. The President enquired with amazement, but in his usual jovial manner, why I was shadowing him. He proceeded to crack a number of jokes with me and even started paying me personal compliments, though his gallantries always remained within the bounds of amiability and good taste.

"You'd better look out, Señorita! We Nicaraguans are mad on blondes, you know!"

He roared with laughter. I retorted coolly:

"I certainly appreciate the courtesy I have met with from the other sex in Nicaragua, but I imagine that Nicaraguan men prefer their blondes to wear skirts and do their hair properly. I doubt if they would care for a bird of passage like myself, especially with a complexion ruined by the sun and wind."

After a few more genial exchanges of this sort I believed I had gained my point. But in the end I had to go without that new weapon I wanted.

Some time later, I passed the house where Ruben Dario, the great Nicaraguan poet, of world-wide reputation, was born. The house had rather a forlorn appearance; chickens were feeding peacefully in the yard. I gave my animals a little rice and reflected for a while on the transitory nature of the fame of even the greatest men; then I rode on towards the frontier of Honduras.

At Somoto I received one of the biggest shocks of my life. I had tethered the animals outside an inn and was asleep, rolled up in my blankets. Suddenly I was awakened by a long-drawn neigh from Fury. It was the kind of neigh that meant serious danger. No wonder—Young Luchador had disappeared. I remembered having seen some men prowling about the place during the afternoon. As always happens, though I then had plenty of time to observe them, I had not noticed their faces. It is also sometimes the case that after the damage has been done we believe we noticed ugly looks among people who looked in fact no better and no worse than others. Anyhow, I mounted Fury immediately and galloped for all I was worth down the only road I could imagine the robbers to have taken. I kept yelling, all the time, Young Luchador's pet name:

"Chiquito! Chiquito!"

All at once I heard his unmistakeable whinny; he had heard my call. I found him standing in the road waiting for me, and threw my arms round his neck in an ecstasy of relief. It was obvious that the robbers had not been able to continue their flight with the animal, which had been doing its best to escape. I remembered that the first of his whinnies I had heard were weak and intermittent, indicating that he had not yet succeeded in freeing himself from the thieves.

After my fright and its happy ending, I left the Republic of Nicaragua, taking with me pleasant memories of those who had been kind and of assistance to me in that country.

CHAPTER XV

CENTRAL AMERICA AND AN INDIAN FESTIVAL

MY journey through Honduras began with a lonely ride downhill over difficult country where I could find no grazing for the horses. I sometimes wondered how my poor animals could stand such hardships, and perhaps if they could think they would also wonder how I could stand them. The tick plague had begun to attack us again and the animals were making themselves positively ill in their nervous exasperation with this wretched parasite. I include myself among its victims, for the cunning little beast had got under my skin and was making my life a perfect misery.

When I reached Tegucigalpa I found myself in trouble with the authorities. The Immigration Department accused me of having broken Honduras law, which only allowed me a stay of forty-eight hours, because I had now been in the country eight days. I told the official who interviewed me that I should like to see the Minister, though I had been informed that this gentleman had a shocking temper. When I called on the Minister that afternoon I found that he and the official who had interviewed me were one and the same person.

On this occasion we got on very well together and the matter of my law-breaking was satisfactorily settled.

When I resumed my route, I met only very poor people who could give me little assistance though I stood in considerable need of it. To add to my troubles the country was in the throes of political elections and in this particular district alcohol was flowing like water and there were constant brawls and riots. Lorryloads of voters were roaming the roads in most truculent fashion. This state of affairs rendered everything far from safe and my chances of finding a lodging for the

153

night in the villages or even somewhere to rest during the day seemed remote. Just as I myself felt nervous in this atmosphere of insecurity, the villagers also appeared rather nervous of me.

My ride through Honduras, where I visited Espino de Choluteca, San Lorenzo de Valle, Nacaome, El Amatillo, Tegucigalpa, the capital, and other places where I was cordially welcomed, put one more stage of the journey behind me and enabled me to come to know yet another beautiful country. The worst conditions I met with were drought and lack of fodder during part of the time. The hunger from which Fury and Young Luchador suffered wrung my heart. The drought obliged me to leave my horses on an estate called Jicarito Comalí in the province of Choluteca, while I paid a necessary visit to Tegucigalpa, the capital. I caused the newspapers, *La Epoca* and *El Pueblo*, in that city to record the fact, so that no movement either by myself or my horses should remain unaccounted for during the period of the ride.

My first few days in the Republic of Salvador passed off excellently; everyone seemed to know all about me and to be anxious to entertain me. I could not enjoy this hospitality for long, as it could not follow me and my horses over the long stretches of open country and desert I had to traverse. We suffered chiefly, on this part of the journey, from the stifling heat. Over one desolate and barren tract the sun blazed down with such crushing power that our mouths seemed full of tinder and our veins of fire.

I was obliged to roll up my trousers in order to prevent the fabric burning my legs when it stuck to my knees on account of the profuse perspiration induced. This expedient let me in for a rather disagreeable, though somewhat comic, incident. I was passing a detachment of mounted police in uniform and one of them seemed to think that I ought not to be going about with partly bare legs. He blew his whistle shrilly and then, as I simply rode on, seized the reins of my horse, tugging at them with some violence. Some passers-by collected to listen to my argument with the policeman, though I doubt if they were much edified by it. The man appeared to wish to arrest me. I shouted at him: "Arrest me, then, if you're man enough to do it!"

In spite of all this fuss nothing, in the end, happened. I arrived at San Salvador, capital of the Republic, with my knees still bare to the sun and the wind.

Shortly afterwards the President of the Republic, Lieutenant-Colonel Oscar Osorio, received me. Somehow or other he had heard of my remorseless but ineffectual persecution of President Somoza of Nicaragua with the object of inducing him to present me with a revolver, which in the end I never obtained. I explained to Colonel Osorio:

"Your Excellency, I'm not always such a nuisance, you know."

"Well, you won't have to be, here," he said. "What sort of weapon would you like?"

"A long .38 would be splendid."

"Very well, you shall have one."

He was as good as his word. I received this efficient weapon, together with a good supply of ammunition.

In Salvador a rather curious episode occurred. A certain married couple took to preceding me through the cities of the country, boasting of a number of extraordinary feats. On occasions the woman represented herself as having been despatched by Argentine sporting circles to ride through America. They were always turning up unexpectedly on my route, either following or preceding me. They took no notice of my protests that I did not need an escort and ignored my requests that they should leave me alone. Their interference went on so long and reached such proportions that I could not prevent the Press and the diplomatic authorities from taking a hand in the game.

The couple, who had more money than sense, seemed to think that such trips as mine, long or short, on horseback, could be performed in luxurious fashion. They often took the train, or else went by air. They rode mainly when their arrival in a city might be productive of publicity.

The couple in question were Barbarita Ricci and her husband Miguel, and for some time they shadowed me wherever they could and managed to turn up wherever I went.

The First Secretary of the Argentine Embassy, Señor José Palmentieri, communicated an announcement to the Press, which I read in the *Tribuna Libre*. It was worded as follows:

"I have the honour to beg the Editor to be so good as to give adequate publicity in the distinguished periodical he controls to the following explanation of the article published on page 2 of the current issue referring to the horsewoman, Barbarita Ricci, as an Argentine citizen and as having begun her ride from Buenos Aires in the Republic of Argentina in the month of August 1948, in company with her husband Miguelito Ricci, also said to be an Argentine citizen. I would beg you to be so good as to take note that the said Señora Barbarita Ricci is neither an Argentine citizen nor did she leave Argentina to undertake the ride in question. The only Argentine lady who did so is Señorita Ana Beker. My object in submitting this explanation to the Editor is to prevent any person utilising alleged Argentine nationality to undermine the good faith of the citizens and representatives of the Government or Press of Salvador, from thereby pursuing gainful ends. In thanking the Editor for his kind co-operation in this matter I take this opportunity of conveying to him my most profound and respectful greetings."

I immediately forgot this annoying affair and left San Salvador, making straight for the frontier. At Santa Ana, close to the border, I rested on a sugar-plantation owned by a Spaniard, before entering Guatemala.

I crossed into this country by way of San Cristobal and pressed on through Asunción, Mita, Jutiapa and Barbarena, riding in the direction of the capital along a road which was occasionally paved and for considerable distances ran to quite a good surface.

I was received in the capital by the Argentine ambassador, Señor Mariscoti, and interviewed by representatives of *Life* and *Time* who told me they would prefer to question me after my arrival in the United States.

The first day I spent in Guatemala city happened to be Students' Day, when the young people are allowed complete liberty to say, sing and write anything they please. They take full advantage of the concession, making the most reckless jests about and attacks on public institutions, statesmen and administrative officers; the license only lasted a day and all such behaviour was tolerated out of respect for tradition.

As I travelled up through the Republic towards Mexico I made some interesting contacts with the aboriginals; in some villages they treated me with something like veneration and followed me about everywhere.

I began to approach the most mountainous and forbidding territory in Guatemala as I still had to score a final victory over the giddy precipices of Central America.

A number of the aboriginals offered to guide me and for several days I especially enjoyed the company of one of them; he was a hale old fellow, a great lover of his country and very knowledgeable about it. While the horses and I leapt across one yawning gap after another or put ourselves to rights after falling down a cliff, he talked to me as though to a foreigner whom it amused him to instruct. He told me that the antiquity of the Guatemalan race far exceeded that of most other peoples. The oldest of them, he said, came originally from the valley of the river Usumacinta in Mexico. Then there were the Quechuans, who were as ancient as the Mayas. He assured me that he could read the hieroglyphics carved on the stone ruins and understood in its purest form the language from which that spoken by the Indians of to-day had been derived.

He referred in phrases of reverent and warm affection to the relics of antique Guatemalan civilisation, to the colossal statues of Quirigua, the mysterious inscriptions and the ruins in the province of Petén and at Zaculeu. I took the opportunity to inspect such monuments of the past when I passed through Huehuetenango.

My elderly guide praised the ingenuity and wealth which must have been required to enable that ancient race to succeed in transporting stones of such tremendous size from the quarries and placing them in position. To hear him talk, one would have believed the civilisation of his ancestors, in their forests, to have been one of dazzling splendour. He said they had measured the duration of the year before the Romans did and instituted an efficient calendar; that they calculated the equinoxes and had invented the figure nought before any of the oriental civilisations; yet they had known nothing of the wheel or of mining or of many other techniques fundamental to the development of humanity.

The aboriginals I met mostly belonged to the Quiché race, though there were many other branches, such as the Cakchiquel, Uspantec, Lacandon, Mam, Pokoman and Tzendal stocks.

Just as my guide was beginning to give me an account of the ancient splendours of the Quiché kingdom, Fury slipped and sent a big rock hurtling down a steep gradient. The horse fell with the boulder and when we went down to rescue him he was snorting wildly and kicking out with all four legs as if he couldn't get up. It took us quite a time to haul him to his feet and replace his saddle and harness.

After this my informant resumed his tale, referring to a certain King Kikab who had led his armies as far as Nicaragua. I had to take leave now of this venerable chronicler of old Guatemala; I was to miss him on such occasions as that when I crossed the region called Los Chocollos which was said to be infested with brigands. I don't know how much truth there was in the rumour, nor if the fellow I met was in fact a bandit, but the fact is that one day when I was feeling utterly worn out with climbing up and climbing down, riding first in one direction and then in another, I did meet a man who looked very much like one. If the fellow had been following me during my recent manœuvres, he would certainly have had pity on me and left me alone; the road in this part of Guatemala was like a switchback, up hill and down dale, and as tortuous as a maze.

This individual looked extremely shabby and far from prepossessing of feature. He yelled at me:

"Get off that horse! Hurry up! Come on!"

"Why? What for?"

"That's my business!"

I remembered my revolver was not loaded, so I pretended I was going to pull up and obey the man, but instead of doing so I suddenly put both horses into a fast trot, riding far enough away to give me time to take three cartridges from the clip and load them in the chamber; as soon as I had done so, I let the fellow come up.

"Halt, there!" I ordered him. "Put up your hands. It's the last thing you'll ever do!"

If he'd known how frightened I was, in spite of my threatening appearance, he might perhaps have plucked up courage, but as it was he lost heart altogether and merely mumbled in a quavering tone: "Are you going to kill me?"

"Not if you clear out quick!"

He did clear out, as fast as his legs would carry him, but only to hide beyond a bend in the road, in case there should be a chance of confronting me again. By this time, however, I had loaded all six cartridges in my revolver and was determined not to let my fright get the better of me.

I rode on, skirting the edge of a precipice, keeping both horses under control with one hand and holding my weapon ready in the other. The man appeared again, following me, but I could not understand what he was after. He stopped a few yards away and called out:

"If you want to kill me, go ahead!"

I was far from wanting to do any such thing and now felt much calmer. My revolver was fully loaded and the *machete* I had seen in his belt the first time I caught sight of him could not be compared with my own weapon for efficiency.

My assailant, if he can be called that, changed his tactics. He informed me that he had a shed in which my horses could be stabled and added a lot of other improbable statements which reeked of lies improvised on the spur of the moment. I again ordered him, with threats, to take himself off and not to dare to come near me, whereupon he once more retreated, but only to go and hide among some bushes. I then fired without, of course, intending to hit him. I heard him running away. Apparently this time he was making off for good.

I put the revolver back in its holster after a time, considering that I had now done with this persistent individual.

In one of the surrounding groves I saw for the first time the beautiful bird called the quetzal. In full flight it looked to me like a flashing jewel. The brilliant gold, ruby and emerald of its plumage render it one of the most colourful and lovely of birds. The scarlet of its breast-feathers is the source of a legend still current among the local Indians, that in the days of King Tecun, when that king was engaged in mortal combat with Pedro de Alvarado, the Spanish *conquistador*, the quetzal, acting as Tecun's guardian angel, tried to peck out the eyes of the Christian invader and, when the latter had slain the Quiché king, bathed its breast in the blood of the conquered hero. It is perhaps for this reason that the quetzal figures in the national coat of arms of Guatemala.

The sumptuous natural beauty of this tropical landscape, where man's handiwork seems hung amid the gigantic achievement of nature includes one of the loveliest of flowers, the *Monja Blanca* (White Nun), which is regarded as an emblem of the country. It is a species of orchid, the colour of white marble, or of the most delicately smooth skin that can be imagined.

I continued my search for the way out of Guatemala. I had a small map with me on which I had noted the places I ought to pass through after leaving Huehuetenango; I often made such notes, though I generally had to modify them in accordance with the actual character of the route. In this case my note read: 'Itinerary to Mexican frontier: Stage 1, San Rafael Petzal, find Ezequiel Aguirre. Stage 2, follow road as far as Chimique, then turn right to San Pedro Necta, where contact mayor. Stage 3, La Democracia, where contact mayor or the widow Sofia Galvez de Argueta. Stage 4, essential to find La Mesilla. Call Guatemala Travel Agency and El Jocote Travel Agency for Mexico.'

These were the sort of notes I had to guide me; it often happened, however, that they did not include extremely important information, as for instance how to cross a river which I might unexpectedly find across my path.

At San Pedro Necta, a place which can only be reached by travelling across ruggedly mountainous country, I found a local festival going on and was invited to take part in it, an experience I shall never forget. Since I had entered Bolivia and Peru I had several times been present at dances, dramatic spectacles, traditional processions, carnivals and so on, but I had never yet so much admired the picturesque splendour of the costumes and ornaments and the superb dancing which lent an incomparable vivacity to the scene. The celebrations lasted for several days. The most important of the mimed plays represented battles of long ago between the natives of the country and the Spanish invaders. The dancers wore masks, embroidered jackets, helmets and plumes of feathers as they performed, to the music of oboes, evolutions imitative of ancient encounters with the Spaniards, in addition to such well-established traditional dances of Guatemala as the *tun* or *venado*. The headman paid me constant attentions and presented me with an entire costume of great magnificence of the kind worn by Indian women at these festivals. The Guatemalan aboriginals, I must say, treated me in general as one of themselves, although I was an Argentine.

The women kept their eyes fixed on me with frank curiosity and overwhelmed me with questions. The men concentrated their admiration on the powerful build and size of the horses and asked my permission to mount them with the phrase:

"May I borrow your ladder?"

San Pedro Necta was one of the most charming and picturesque villages I visited during the whole of my ride; it can meet every conceivable requirement of the tourist. The large Indian population and the character of the landscape seem to remove it altogether from the familiar uniformity of modern civilization. The only trouble is the difficulty of transport in such a remote region, which for all practical purposes can only be explored on foot or mule.

The headman appointed a guide to accompany me—it was just as well that he did so, for the last stage of my journey through Guatemala to the Mexican frontier proved perfectly fiendish. I use the word to describe the nature of the country, even after all my experiences of regions wild and forbidding to a degree, because it was some of the worst going that I had yet encountered.

Those last strenuous days of my ride through Guatemala were spent hanging on to Young Luchador's tail; he had grown quite accustomed to leaping like a deer over rocks and gullies. We crossed suspension bridges made of wire and boards, which were not intended to take any animal heavier or bulkier than a small donkey. My two horses were fated to negotiate obstacles which would not have been out of place in a circus of trick riders.

On the point of crossing into Mexico I was confronted by the problem of avoiding Tapachula, where the first Mexican Customs post was situated. I had been told that the Customs authorities there were rather fussy and required a deposit of 200 dollars for every horse brought into the country; it was essential for me to avoid this expense for my financial resources were as shaky as ever.

At the Mexican frontier the Inter-American Highway, which is called Roosevelt Road in Guatemala, and Christopher Columbus Road in Mexico, ceases to exist for a time. Each country builds its own part of the road in the direction it considers the right one; the two directions do not coincide. The Mexicans say that the Guatemalans are building in the wrong direction and the Guatemalans say the same about the Mexicans. When I turned off the road for the reasons just mentioned I had once more to traverse terribly rugged country. The road only ran from Guatemala to Tapachula and there stopped dead, or at any rate it did so at the period of my ride. Motorists proceeding by that route were obliged to take their cars on by train if they wished to go any further.

I now had to find my way to another long stretch of that famous Inter-American Highway, which I had been following with my two four-footed companions almost continuously along its winding course throughout Central America. Starting practically at sea-level in Panama, it rises gradually as far as David, reaches a height of over 3,000 feet at Volcán and then makes a series of steep descents to Buenos Aires. It ascends to about 12,000 feet between San Isidro del General and Cartago and climbs very high again to San Ramón on the Nicaraguan-Honduras frontier, and on to Chimaltenago and San Cristobal. Then it descends once more as it approaches the Mexican border, where it completes a total length of some 1,750 miles.

My horses and I were accompanied for the first stage of our ride through Mexico by an Indian guide, as otherwise we should have been hopelessly lost in that trackless and mountainous wilderness. I entered the land of the Aztecs by way of a region lying between Cuouhtemoc and Motozintio. Before reaching the first towns of any importance I endured one of the severest ordeals of my whole ride. It was mountainous country all the time, very hot, and I found hardly anything for us to eat. But by this time I had grown physically used to frequent fasting. To spend a day and a night without a morsel of food passing my lips was nothing to me. Sometimes in the course of the ride I did not eat for as many as four days running.

Even when I had a certain amount of money on me and was passing places where I might have bought food I did not always do so, as I preferred to reserve my slender funds to buy fodder for the horses. Their hunger presented me with more serious and pressing problems than my own. I also gave preference to expenditure on obtaining a night's lodging when the weather was exceptionally bad. In densely populated areas and those where I was frequently offered hospitality I kept my appetite in check until I was invited to satisfy it.

CHAPTER XVI

MY INVASION OF MEXICO

A T Tuxla in Mexico I suddenly realised that the horses could not go on with the new saddles I had ordered for them in Guatemala; their backs were swollen and they were suffering agonies from the chafing. The District Governor, a doctor-of-law named Efrain Aranda Osorio, came providentially to my rescue.

I stayed in Tuxla eight days during which I was invited to a most charming entertainment in a small village in the mountains. There were fireworks and much singing of the Mexican and Argentine national anthems. Before I left, the governor presented me with a chestnut horse named Dragon, to ride while the other two recovered from the sores inflicted by the saddles. He was an excellent animal and I am grateful both to him and to the Governor for their help, but I never regarded him as more than a temporary substitute I should dismiss as soon as he had served his auxiliary purpose. I wanted to finish my ride with my two original companions.

But soon the echoes of the songs and other compliments paid me died away and I set off once more.

At five in the morning I left the village where I had been so hospitably entertained and rode on till eight in the evening. The atmosphere and my own feelings went steadily from bad to worse. The effects of the heat were aggravated by a shortage of water that drove me to despair; I was reduced to drinking from filthy ponds. Whenever, at long intervals, I caught sight of one of those great wagons drawn by several pairs of oxen, I never failed to ask for a drink and also to be allowed to take with me some of the water they carried.

I was feeling extremely thirsty and in a very bad temper when a sergeant of the mounted police with exceptionally huge moustaches commanded me, in a peremptory tone, to halt.

"Show me your passport. If it's not perfectly in order, you don't go a step further."

I knew well enough that at the place near El Ocotal where I had entered the country no passports of any kind were either issued or regularised. No one could have done such a thing except some stray Indian muleteer or one of the lizards that darted about among the bushes on the mountainside.

"The object of my journey has been duly authorised and I don't need a passport."

"I don't care what the object of your journey may be. You are a traveller like anyone else—though you don't look like anyone else."

"Don't you ever read newspapers or listen to the radio? Don't you know who I am?"

"So far as I am concerned you are a woman with three horses. As you observe, I am still able to notice the difference."

"What about the difference between some people and a donkey?" I demanded, losing all patience.

We went on arguing like this for some time. The man with the moustaches obstinately declined to believe that any official authority, Government or diplomatic body could be interested in or make an exception in favour of a madwoman like myself who roamed about in semi-fancy dress on the worst roads she could find.

I showed him my route-book, pointing to the signatures and testimonials it contained, some of which were stamped at the bottom with the eagle-and-serpent seal of the United States of Mexico.

In the end, after declaring that he himself would never dream of signing such a book if the bearer did not produce a passport, he allowed me to go my way though he warned me that he would report the matter to higher authority and I should probably be arrested before I went much further.

No one, however, arrested me just then. I was pursued, all the same, and mercilessly persecuted by thirst, as I pushed on through wild, barren and precipitous country.

My horses, those faithful companions for so many weeks and months, gazed at me with a mute question in their eyes, as though they were reproaching me for that endless series of stony hills and valleys, where they continually lost their footing and had to struggle so cruelly. Sometimes they came to a complete standstill, as if begging me, with every sign of genuine exhaustion, to put a stop to it all. I was obliged to encourage them with words of which they understood only the heartening intention.

Both animals suffered in the same way, but they both reacted differently; their characters were not at all alike. Fury resembled a sensitive young aristocrat, very fond of his own comfort. He hated mud, even if it only splashed him, to an exaggerated degree. The slightest inconvenience irritated him. Young Luchador, on the other hand, had much more of the long-suffering peasant in him. He could put up with anything and showed great pertinacity in seeking out the safest footholds and refuges from danger.

But it is worth while, in Mexico, to endure almost any vexation and toil in order to be compensated by the solicitude of a people whose chivalrous disposition is beyond praise; they are true brothers of the *gaucho*, and great gentlemen. I shall always remember the amateur riders of Mexico and the generous hospitality I enjoyed in Mexican clubs and at the meetings of various societies. It was in the State of Puebla that I was first entertained in this way. In all towns where such clubs existed I was declared their guest or that of the Tourist Office. I used to be met, before I reached the place, by an elegant cavalcade which escorted me with the utmost dash and brilliance.

I was immensely delighted when I saw Mexican horsemen for the first time in their characteristic garb of wide-brimmed, high-crowned hats, extremely short glittering jackets and full, belted trousers, lavishly adorned with buttons. I later examined with much interest the unusual type of saddle used, very different from the *gaucho* outfit and that of the country people generally in Argentina, as well as the exceptionally long stirrups.

With these accoutrements, which the Mexicans call *pilchas*, I saw them carry out the most dexterous and daring evolutions at the equestrian entertainments given in my honour. I was particularly impressed by their horsemanship after I had watched them bring down young bulls by roping them round the hind legs.

Apart from these equestrian displays I also enjoyed at Puebla the traditional festive gatherings so typical of the country and so vivacious in their gaiety. I drank the national beverage, *pulque*, as I watched the fun and dancing, admiring especially the *zapateado*, or tap-dancing, carried out by the experts in this line.

On leaving Puebla, where I had been received by the State Governor, I was accompanied for about two hours by these gay cavaliers, who showed me a road which saved me several miles of my journey. Eventually, however, I found myself alone once more.

I rode on deep in thought, recalling all sorts of recent episodes and encounters, even of the sentimental kind, for I had met a certain gentleman near Puebla who proposed marriage to me. I told him, however, that I believed he was merely giving expression to an impulsive ardour of the moment and that my own sentiments were exclusively devoted to the task of continuing and completing my ride, from which no other consideration could divert me.

I had put my revolver in my bag while I was riding about with the local cavaliers, as I did not want to make a parade of being armed on such occasions, or when entering a city; I now replaced the weapon in my belt. However, as the water I had recently drunk was disagreeing with me, and I had a stomach-ache, I found the weight of the revolver in that position a nuisance. I put it back for the time being in the bag, never dreaming that the action would have such dismal consequences for me.

After my escort had left me to myself and I was still riding on through the State of Puebla, I came to a very deep ravine. A vague foreboding, one of those sudden presentiments of evil that one can never account for, caused me to draw rein.

My two horses also seemed to share my uneasiness. I say 'two', for I had been obliged to leave Dragon, the chestnut presented to me as already recorded, at Puebla, in the care of the military garrison. He was by that time exhausted and in no condition to carry on with the others on my journey, in which, after all, his participation had been almost negligible.

I told myself that the ravine was only 'one more of those hollows' and rode on. But as soon as we were well into it I suddenly heard a loud, harsh shout of "Halt! Where are you going?"

I saw two men dressed in the usual fashion of that part of the country, wearing very wide-brimmed hats. They had the grim features, dark olive complexions and lank black hair so common in the rural districts of Mexico; both had drawn revolvers. One seized the bridle of my horse. My first thought was to draw my own weapon as quickly as I could, but for the reason already given I was unable to do so. The best I could do was to try to move nearer to the pack-horse, but the men prevented me from doing so by levelling their revolvers in a manner which left me no choice but to obey. One of them said: "We are police officers. Show us your baggage."

I hid my fear, and retorted, with the energy I can usually command in a crisis, though I cannot imagine where it comes from:

"You're robbers. Fine lot of policemen you are!"

I wished they had been the police; as a rule they were always on my side.

While one of the men kept me covered with his revolver the other put his hand in the bag attached to my saddle. He fished out a number of articles which he contemplated with great satisfaction. They included my revolver, the camera I had bought in Bolivia, the silk scarf which was part of my gaucho outfit and a big Argentine flag. He also took from my saddlebag a wallet with a hundred Mexican pesos in it.

While he was doing this I noticed a third man, who was watching the scene from the other side of the ravine. I called to him at the top of my voice.

"Come here, my friend! Come and look what they're doing! Can't you help me? Can't you go and tell someone?"

He walked towards us with a smile I did not like the look of and a confident gesture of greeting, not addressed to me but to the others, who were doubtless his cronies.

"Another brigand, eh?" I remarked. None of the three men took the slightest notice of this observation.

That was not the only insulting name I called him. But the three of them coolly went on taking possession of the articles from my bag. My *gaucho* silk scarf dropped to the ground and, seeing that for the moment I could do nothing to stop the robbery, since I was covered all the time by the barrels of two revolvers, I exclaimed:

"Why can't you be generous for once in your lives and leave me that scarf, which is no earthly use to you, while I need it as part of my clothing?"

"We can use anything. We've no time to waste, either."

"Take everything else and the money as well, but leave me that scarf," I begged.

In the end they agreed; one of them threw me the scarf.

"That's to show you we're not what we seem and not brigands, as you think."

"Why shouldn't I think so?"

My object in asking this and similar questions was to persuade them to leave me the silk Argentine flag as well. But there was too much silk in that item and they wouldn't hand it over.

They seemed anxious to get away and began uttering threats when they saw that I stayed where I was, staring at them.

"Well, which would you rather do, clear out with a whole skin and keep your mouth shut, or die this minute?"

I had no doubts on the subject at all. The only trouble was, I felt really terrified in case they should fire on me the moment my back was turned.

I set off reluctantly, straining my ears in the expectation of a shot. But it did not come. I was able gradually to gather speed, without looking behind me. I was only too grateful to fate for allowing me to keep the horses, though I did not understand, at the time, the reason why the robbers had not taken them. But I was afterwards told, when I reported the matter, that horses are seldom stolen in such cases because they are easy to trace on account of their colour and other characteristics. My own beasts, moreover, were particularly well known owing to the photographs published in the newspapers.

I decided to return to Puebla to replace so far as possible the property that had been stolen. On arrival I reported the theft to the police. The announcement caused an immediate and widespread sensation throughout the city, especially in riding and Press circles. I was provided with quarters in a hotel and it soon became evident that everyone was anxious to overwhelm me with attentions in order to counteract the effects on my mind of this disagreeable incident.

General Avila Camacho himself, the brother of the President of the Republic, sent for me in order that he might express his sympathy.

"I have just heard the story," he told me, "and am most distressed about it. I like Argentina so much. It is a great country you have left behind you on your gallant journey and I can't tell you how much it grieves me to think that it should have been in Mexico that this dreadful thing happened to you."

The losses I had sustained by the robbery were more than made good by the State authorities of Puebla, mainly those of the Army and Police.

I had reached the city in a car placed at my disposal for the time being, after I had stabled the horses in a small village near the town of Huejotzingo.

The State Governor, General Avila Camacho, as well as receiving me so kindly, as I have just related, had immediately ordered General David Leon Arias, the Chief of Police, to provide me with accommodation in the Royal Hotel and set his men to work to track down the robbers. Two officers and a detachment of police accompanied me to the scene of the crime and were there joined in their investigations by the mayors of Jotzingo and Zacatepec.

Meanwhile the Royal filled up with reporters anxious to obtain details of the hold-up which remained front-page news in Puebla for some days. All the papers carried such headlines as 'Attack on the Argentine Amazon', 'Ana Beker victimised in a daring robbery', 'Stopped by three unidentified individuals near Huejotzingo and robbed of money, pistol and camera'. The *Sol de Puebla* wrote: 'The Argentine Amazon has been robbed. Yesterday she was held up on the road near Huejotzingo, soon after she had taken leave of a group of members of the Puebla Cavaliers.' The *Diario de Puebla* announced: 'Hold-up of the Amazon. Three persons laid a trap for her.'

Soon afterwards the *Opinión* and other periodicals printed the following official statement: 'The Governor has reimbursed the lady *gaucho* for all the property she lost in the robbery. As a mark of friendship towards the Argentine nation and its valiant representative, Ana Beker, the famous horsewoman, the Governor of this Community, Rafael Avila Camacho, cordially received the Amazon yesterday, at 8.30 a.m., in his office at Government House. He made good from his private purse the losses which Señorita Beker sustained in the highway robbery which she reported recently to the police. General Avila Comacho expressed to Señorita Beker his profound regret at this disagreeable incident, which occurred while she was riding to Mexico City, and presented her with a camera and a pistol in order to relieve the pressure on her funds.'

This was true and I was extremely grateful for the generous gifts made to me.

Though in a great hurry now to get on to the capital I continued to receive many invitations. Among the entertainments offered me by the General I particularly enjoyed an exhibition provided by a famous horse named *Hidalgo Rojo* ('Red Lord') and his no less famous rider Severiano Hernandez.

By this time I had lost all interest in the question of the 'hold-up'. I wanted to forget it and went so far as to declare that the robbers had treated me with a certain amount of consideration.

A Puebla reporter, when he heard me almost taking the thieves' part, remarked ironically:

"I wonder you didn't make them sign your route-book, if you were so grateful for their kindness!"

Nevertheless, both the municipal authorities and the Press continued to follow the matter up. On the 4th June, 1953 the *Diario* wrote: 'No clue has yet been obtained, either by the Judiciary Police or the Criminal Investigation Department, as to the perpetrators of the shameful attack recently made upon Señorita Ana Beker, the Argentine horsewoman, when three persons robbed her of the money she had with her, as well as of some other articles of personal property, while she was riding along one of the local roads near Huejotzingo. It may be that silence is being maintained in order not to prejudice the work of the police which is still proceeding with a view to discovering the identity of the criminals, arresting them and bringing them to justice.'

Before I left I read another article, which attached a very great deal of importance to the affair. 'The attack on the lady from the Argentine may have serious consequences for the plans under consideration in Puebla for attracting tourists to the city. In the case of a similar attack upon some North Americans at Teotihuacan the opportunity was seized to give vigorous and outspoken publicity to the insinuation that travel is not safe in the Republic. There can be no doubt that the subsequent decline in tourist traffic is partly to be attributed to this cause. The measures taken to ensure public security must be redoubled and the offenders in the present case must be punished. As regards the future, it is equally essential for still more facilities to be offered for travel in Mexico and especially to Puebla. We recommend the Tourist Office to study this problem. The recent outrage may well cancel, at one stroke, the results of all the efforts made and expense incurred by the Municipality in this connection.'

I think myself that it showed excessive though praise-worthy zeal to draw such exaggerated conclusions from the facts as known. I am quite convinced that the crime had no adverse effects on questions of public administration in Puebla or the country as a whole.

Nor do I consider that it was bad advice to take the old

road to Mexico City, which was not macadamised and therefore very good for the horses, as well as being the most direct,
though the lonelier and thus more dangerous of the two.

The Puebla authorities told me that before I left the city
I should have a chance to see once more the brigands who
had held me up. All the same, I did not see them, though I
was shown a great number of persons of doubtful antecedents
who might have been capable of anything.

Chapter XVII

THE MISFORTUNES OF MY TWO HORSES

I REACHED San Martin soon afterwards and was given a tremendous reception; the schoolchildren formed up in a double row and pelted me with flowers. This was to happen several times again on my journey and I had to postpone my schedule to give them an account of what they were pleased to call my 'feats', adventures such as might happen on any prolonged journey. On these occasions, children of both sexes gathered round me and asked all sorts of questions. As the imagination, at this tender age, tends to run to fantasy, many of them only wanted to hear me describe how I had been attacked by wild beasts and brigands and all that sort of thing. After I had finished speaking they often called out "Long live Argentina!" or "Come back, please, Amazon!" clapping their hands very charmingly.

Details of my ride were broadcast by means of loud-speakers. Pretty village girls in picturesque costumes came out to welcome me. In some towns I was given Mexican flags and adorned with paper garlands.

At Aguacaliente, a watering-place, I spent the night in a private house belonging to the amiable Camino family, where I enjoyed one of the most delightful experiences of my whole ride. I was awakened in the morning by voices singing the 'Farmers' Song'. When I opened the window I saw an elegant group of horsemen from the National Cavaliers Federation. They had come to serenade me and see me on my way. I went out to them and kissed the President of the Federation.

But this was only a foretaste of the thrills that were in store for me. When I entered Mexico City, President José

V. Rodriguez informed me that all the citizens were impatient to do me honour. I made the acquaintance of the 'Queen of the Cavaliers', Señorita Maria Beatriz Baldovinos, a most beautiful girl, wearing the typical big Mexican *sombrero*. I also met the Military Attaché of the Argentine Embassy, Colonel Blas Alfredo Lomuto, and his wife Chela.

One Sunday, during my stay in Mexico City, the Regional Cavalier Group, in association with a similar group, who had a secondary interest in wine, invited me to an elaborate festival at the Grand Ranch of the Corporation. The spectacles included every possible sport that could be indulged in at a gathering of skilled horsemen. There was lassoing, trick horsemanship, riding on young bulls, the 'death gallop' and other exhibitions of equestrian dexterity, as well as characteristic Mexican dancing, the *floreos*, the *haraba*, the *tapatillo* and so on.

Perhaps the highlight of all these festivities was the rustic banquet, in traditional Argentine style, given by the Argentine Embassy to the cavaliers of the Federal District in return for the hospitality extended to myself. At the estate of Coyoacan, where I was staying, the Embassy collected a colourful assembly, the brilliant dresses of the ladies being designed by the famous rider Antonio Teran, Rogelio Martinez and myself. The wife of the Argentine ambassador, Señora Tezanos Pinto, was present.

My enthusiasm, ever since infancy, for anything to do with horsemanship ensured my admiration for the skill displayed by the planters in their exercises, lassoing with the scarf, somersaulting, roping from horseback and all the other items of their expert repertory.

I retained a vivid mental picture of all the equestrian spectacles I had witnessed and the varied attractions of the beautiful capital city, including the superb architecture of the Palace of Fine Arts; the Juarez Crescent, built to preserve the immortal memory of that hero; Lake Xochimilco, a romantic sheet of water which I explored in one of the decorative boats that glide over its smooth surface, and all the other outstanding beauty spots I visited.

After leaving Mexico City I rode on northwards through an almost uniformly barren countryside, with little water or grazing for the animals. The unfortunate creatures share all our misfortunes and yet cannot participate to the extent that we can in the pleasures to be derived from a warm welcome. Still, in the absence of any such moral relief, they do at least physically enjoy a good manger and good stabling.

Some forty miles south of Victoria a number of the local horsemen were waiting for me with plenty of fodder for my companions and music to cheer us all up.

The music made me forget another disagreeable incident that had recently occurred. Two exceedingly unpleasant-looking characters had accosted me in a most insolent manner, demanding water. Their request, made to a rider like myself, who obviously had nothing of the kind to offer, was the height of absurdity. This time I had my revolver handy and fully loaded. I told them bluntly: "This is all I have for you."

So saying, I covered them with the weapon; just the opposite had occurred in this case to what had happened as I left Puebla. In other words, it was I who held the whiphand and it was the robbers' turn to be discomfited. All the same, I fired twice in the air to show that I was quite capable of defending myself. I afterwards heard that the men were casual footpads, forest thieves of the type known as 'wet backs', who cross to the United States by swimming and are sent back by the authorities there in lorries.

The Victoria papers, which were most kind to me, and also the Press in other cities, gave a most flattering description of this second attack made upon me in Mexico, alleging that I had driven off my assailants by revolver fire. But actually, to be quite accurate, I merely covered them and thus caused them to abandon their intentions.

Big headlines in the Tampico papers announced: 'The Amazon in a shooting affray', and went on to affirm that one of the 'wet backs' had been seriously wounded and left a trail of blood behind him, though subsequently all trace of him had been lost. As I was certain the shots I had fired in the air could not have hit anyone I supposed the man had been wounded in a fight with one of his companions or with the police who were hunting down these brigands.

At Victoria I was welcomed by demonstrations in my honour such as I had experienced at other places in Mexico. There were similar brilliant equestrian festivals, processions accompanied by the entire population, with the municipal band at their head, gala decorations in the streets, as for a carnival, and so on. I was declared the city's guest. The cavaliers of Victoria struck me as first-rate. They were as accomplished riders as those of Mexico City and Puebla. The Rotary Club invited me to a splendid banquet.

I entered the State of Tamaulipas and stayed the night at the Santa Anita ranch, owned by Señor José Sierra Bustamente, where my horses were regaled on sugar-cane, a great treat for them; my journey continued to be a most pleasant one. One of the presents from the Victoria horsemen which I most appreciated was a bagful of white bread they brought me while I was in the Galeana gorge, before I reached the Mesa de Lera. They knew I did not care much for the maize-cake which is the staple food of the country, so they had decided to present me with enough of this simple yet delicious white bread to provide a daily meal.

I was now approaching that great nation, the United States of North America. While I was waiting in Matamorus, close to the frontier, for the necessary formalities of entry into the States to be completed, a prominent local landowner offered me accommodation in his house and my horses the run of his paddocks and stables, where they would be treated as though they were the property of a king. He kept his word, to begin with, in exemplary fashion, and I felt very deeply grateful to him. He assured me in the warmest terms that he would continue to look after my horses in this way for so long as it might take me to comply with the requirements of the United States authorities.

My dealings with the latter make quite an interesting story. I called on the Texas Immigration Officer with my passport and without a word of preliminary warning he informed me:

"You can't enter the United States as you are not travelling for purposes of sport."

"WHAT?" I gazed at him in utter stupefaction.

"You intend to give lectures, engage in propaganda and raise money."

"I?"

"Yes. You will be living at the country's expense."

"But how can I give lectures if I can't speak a word of English?"

"That doesn't matter. There's no need to argue about it or show me documents. You won't be allowed in."

After taking every step open to me in Matamorus I eventually succeeded in obtaining letters from the Governor and the Emigration Police in Mexico City. Armed with these documents I drove up to the frontier post in a car lent me by a Mexican lady. No sooner had I reached the Mexican end of the bridge than a policeman of the Emigration Service spotted me, bore down on me like a thunderbolt, snatched open the door of the car and hauled me unceremoniously out.

"Didn't you hear me tell you you're not to come this way? Look, there's the road to Mexico!"

"What right have you got to——"

"I've told you already, that's the way to Mexico. Come on, don't try any funny business." He continued to grip me by the arm.

"I'll scream for help in a minute and you'll see they'll let me through!"

"You can scream as much as you like. You won't do any good here."

Nothing I could say would induce them to let me cross the bridge.

Leaving my two horses in the care of the person already mentioned, I returned to Mexico City by bus, having been told by the United States Consulate that they could do nothing for me, as my case fell entirely within the province of the Immigration authorities. Even in the capital itself the United States consul informed me that he was very sorry to hear of my predicament but that he had no power to help me out of it.

Meanwhile, in Matamorus, vigorous protests were being made against my treatment by the frontier officials. There was general condemnation of the pretexts advanced to prevent my continuing my journey over this important stage.

A spokesman of the United States Immigration Service had announced that permission to enter the country had been refused to the Argentine horsewoman Ana Beker because she was not in possession of the requisite funds and might therefore become a charge on the public purse. But, it was objected, she had been counting on her legal passport to enable her to remain in the United States for at least twelve months and yet for some inexplicable reason the Immigration authorities of the city of Brownsville declined to admit her. In consequence, it went on, the 'famous horsewoman was compelled, yesterday, to return to Mexico City by passenger road transport. Ana Beker has shown the editors of local newspapers the passport granted her by the Consulate of the United States for the Federal District of Mexico, with a visa entitling her to residence in the United States during the month of July 1953 and thereafter until the month of July 1954'.

Cables from the United Press and other agencies began to pour in. Public indignation grew steadily more intense.

But in the course of time a far more tragic misfortune befell me than the unjust refusal of the Texas Immigration authorities to permit me to continue my journey northwards. I have already mentioned that my horses were being looked after at this time by a certain landowner, at his own request. Nearly three months went by before at last I found a moment's breathing-space to go and see my animals. I was confident that I should find them in first-rate condition.

On making enquiries for them at the house of the merchant in question it was a great surprise to me to learn that they were no longer in the paddocks and stables placed at their disposal when I last saw them. I was even more astonished at the brusque and disagreeable tone in which the formerly amiable señor answered my questions.

"Oh, your horses? Yes, I sent them off to another pasture,

179

some way from here. They ought to be still there—unless
something has happened to them meanwhile."

I felt an indescribable pang of foreboding.

"I'd like to see them, then, please."

"Well, as I told you, the place is some way off."

"All the same, I'd like to see them. To-day if possible."

"You could only get there by lorry."

"Have a lorry brought round at once then, please."

But the wretched fellow paid no attention to my request.
I had to apply to some friends at a club in Matamorus, who
put a lorry at my disposal to take me to the place, some thirty
miles away, where the merchant had told me the horses now
were. "I may as well tell you," he remarked, as the lorry
started, "that the animals are pretty weak. They seemed to
get depressed when you went away and wouldn't eat."

I knew very well that horses, however much they may
regret the absence of a beloved owner, will never deprive
themselves of food for that reason, if food is made available
for them. In their case eating is a practically mechanical
process in which the mood of the moment plays no part.

We duly reached the place in question, a piece of waste
ground. The horses were there. But I could not begin to
describe their appearance. I could hardly recognise my dear
Fury and Young Luchador, they looked so lean, unkempt and
dirty, nothing but skin and bone. You could count their
ribs. When they saw me they stretched out their necks,
though they could barely manage to make the movement and
uttered not so much a neigh as a feeble moan.

They were tethered by short halters, or they would have
been lying down. Young Luchador had a swollen belly.
There was a pool of filthy water near by; they had not even
the strength to approach it.

I went up to the starving animals and fondled the brittle
hair of their hides and their almost fleshless bones. Their very
eyes were practically blind with accumulated dust and rheum.

Trembling with rage and grief for my poor companions, I
repressed my sobs and had them lifted into the lorry. In the
process Young Luchador fell to the ground.

I could no longer restrain my tears and burst into a wild fit of weeping. Those two beloved and affectionate beings, so generous to me with their loyalty and strength, had been brought to the verge of death by the vile, cowardly treatment to which they had been subjected.

I learned later that at one time the animals had been turned into the street, where they wandered about for some time, tormented by hunger and thirst, pushing at the doors of houses and thrusting their muzzles over the threshold in dumb entreaty for a little water. Little boys threw stones at them and teased them in various other ways. The poor animals ran a very great risk of being picked up by the authorities as useless strays and carried off to the slaughter-house to serve as food for the carnivorous animals in the zoological gardens.

As may be imagined, I did not hesitate to tell the wretch responsible for this foul cruelty exactly what I thought of him. Beside myself with fury at his baseness I loaded him with insults.

"You vile criminals!" I yelled at him and those of his minions who had taken part in the persecution of my unhappy beasts. I could not have hated them more if I myself had been their victim.

I learned that this gentleman's change of attitude towards my horses had been due to his discovery that I was not to be allowed to enter the United States. When he heard, later on, that this decision had been reversed the damage had already been done and could not be repaired. So he sent the animals out of the way to the place where I eventually found them.

A Spanish gentleman, Señor Barrera, at once took charge, in the most kindly manner, of Young Luchador and Fury.

When this dreadful conduct came to the knowledge of the Press and public of Matamorus a tremendous outcry arose. His behaviour had been in direct opposition to the generosity and hospitality which are such conspicuous traits of the Mexican character, and the fact that he had treated a woman in this fashion made matters even worse. *El Bravo*, a periodical that well deserves its name, devoted entire columns to a truly gallant and uncompromising condemnation of his conduct.

A storm of recrimination, taking the forms both of stern and indignant rebuke and of ridicule, witticism and caricature, descended upon the villain. He was bombarded by ten-line epigrams and long satiric poems. *El Bravo*, on the 7th December, published a big caricature showing a Mexican rustic handing over a couple of horses to the gentleman in question with the words: "I should like you to look after these horses for me . . . but please remember I'm not from the Argentine."

The municipality of Matamorus assumed responsibility both for my own maintenance and for that of my animals until we left for North America. Many other local residents were also very kind to me, including Señor Ariola, the aviator, and his wife.

When at last all the problems that had arisen with regard to my crossing of the frontier had been settled, the Stock Breeders' Board carried its inspection of my horses into such meticulous detail as to discover that Fury had only been partially castrated. This caused yet another delay. The Board's veterinary surgeon sent a sample of Fury's blood to Washington to enable the authorities there to decide, by analysing it, whether the animal was capable of siring offspring.

After this question, too, had been satisfactorily answered, my departure from Matamorus took place in style. I started from the Town Hall, accompanied by the Municipal Band and drummers provided by the University students. During the final ceremony my landowner friend attempted to induce me to make up our quarrel and let bygones be bygones. I refused to listen to him. My anger at the suffering he had caused to the beings I loved best in the world had not been appeased. If I could ever have reconciled myself to it I would by this time have forgotten all my resentment. Very likely the gentleman we have been discussing at such length had heard the story put about by the agent at the Information Office, believed what he heard and behaved as he did in order to keep in with his friends across the border.

But his conduct was an isolated case. In general I have nothing but praise for the amicable atmosphere in which I found myself in Mexico. As for the physical atmosphere, the climate itself, that, too, I found to be benevolently disposed to me. There were, of course, a few exceptions, such as the fearful heat in Chuluteca, where I was obliged to travel at night and rest during the day. After all, however troublesome heat may be, it does allow one, at nightfall, to sleep out in the open with one's beasts. But heat can be an awful nuisance, one of its most distressing features being the lack of water which nearly always accompanies it.

CHAPTER XVIII

THE INHOSPITABLE INNKEEPER

AT last I had reached the frontier itself. I crossed at Rio Bravo. Journalists and members of the broadcasting organisation accompanied me to the Immigration Office. I solved the problem of showing that I possessed enough dollars to meet my expenses in the United States as others have done before me. I played a small trick which I consider pardonable in the case of one like myself, invariably short of money and desirous above all of resuming my journey. One can always find someone ready to lend dollars to persons who don't possess them who can thus show them at the right moment and immediately afterwards return them, with commission, to the lender.

As soon as I came in contact with United States citizens I found my ignorance of the language a nuisance. The only reply I could make at first to the endless stream of questions I was asked for the whole of the rest of my ride was to present a written paper.

The crossing of bridges, with their dense traffic and confusing multiplicity of signs, was destined to land me, repeatedly, in awkward situations. The horses were continually rearing, especially Fury, Young Luchador being much more docile, quiet and sensible. I always had to watch Fury very carefully. Sometimes, when I was completely hemmed in by traffic, I used to wave a red scarf as a danger signal to oncoming vehicles.

I had no sooner entered North American territory than I realised that I had found a perfect paradise of intelligent co-operation and helpful organization. Getting into the country had been a most laborious business, but once there my path proved smooth and the inhabitants both kindly and helpful.

This first State, that of Texas, recalls Mexico and South America in its general aspect, but it is organised on wholly North American lines. I often met people who put themselves at my disposal with the greatest courtesy, to escort and help me in any way they could. Oscar del Castillo, editor of the Spanish Section of the *Texas Herald*, gave me very great assistance in this way.

Owing to what had occurred in Matamorus the horses were not yet quite fit enough to proceed and I therefore had to stay where I was for a fortnight. I was very well looked after during this period by the President of the Lions Club, an institution devoted to international solidarity, which resembles in some respects a Rotary Club.

I celebrated the New Year at Harlingen in the cheerful company of some young United Press reporters and members of the television and radio services. I can never thank them all enough, in particular the gentlemen of the United Press.

From the moment I entered Texas I was followed almost everywhere by cameramen and offered every inducement to lead a life of leisure in strong contrast to that which my readers now know so well from descriptions in the previous chapters. Occasionally I was given a police escort, composed of the most amiable wearers of uniform imaginable.

I was offered two thoroughbred horses of the type raised in the great Texan pastures. They were splendid animals but I had to decline the generous offer.

"I would not abandon Young Luchador and Fury for anything in the world," I said. "Not even in exchange for the two finest horses owned by any of the kings of Arabia. Those two companions of mine have faced with me the worst hardships of my ride. It is the dearest wish of my heart to keep them with me till I reach my destination."

"But you ought to accept the offer of those others," someone suggested. "They're very fine specimens and you could easily sell them, without giving up those you have already."

"I'm afraid I'm not a horse-dealer," I answered with a smile, "only a horsewoman."

I gave the same sort of reply to the representative of a television company who proposed that I should appear in one of its programmes purely for my own benefit and for a high fee.

My decision was not only due to my resolve not to commercialise any aspect of my ride, but also to the repeated warnings I had received from the Immigration Office when that body had taken it into its head that I was only going to the States in order to raise money.

By way of Kennedy, Eleberg, Riviera and Ricardo I eventually reached Kingsville, where the largest stock-breeding estate in the world, Kings Ranch, was situated. Here I was given a resplendent cowboy's outfit and taken out on to the exercise ground to watch some vigorous displays of horsemanship. Mr. Claude Chastaut, manager of the store attached to the huge ranch in question, said I could help myself to anything I liked from his stock. I only had to look at some articles, chamois leather trousers for instance, or some other item of ranchers' equipment, and I was told I could have it. The article was then and there placed in my arms. Actually, I should have been quite content with the mere memory of the day I spent at Kingsville, where I was so hospitably entertained that from the moment I arrived red lights were switched on all along the road leading to the place, to prevent any traffic using it while I was on my way. I did, however, tell my hosts, when they suggested taking my horses to graze and rest in a large paddock close by, that I should prefer to have them under my own observation. I still could not forget my unpleasant experience in Matamorus. In compliance with this request they placed the animals in the garden itself under my windows.

From Kingsville I went on by way of the Nueces and Bishop territories to Corpus Christi, where I spent the whole day in a round of festivities organised by the Press and Radio services.

Then I passed through Sinton, Refugio, Victoria, Edna and El Campo, making for Rosemberg.

By this time both Young Luchador and Fury were directing pleased glances at me. They seemed to be saying: 'What extraordinary vicissitudes one does pass through in this world of people and roads—or the lack of them. Now there are no more mountains where we have to leap like goats and break our noses, no more bridgeless rivers we have to swim till we come within an ace of being drowned. There are no more marshes into which we sink up to our bellies and have to be hauled out with ropes, no more embarkations when we stagger and fall from the platforms like toads off a log, no more periods of starving almost to death and no more of these awful intestinal pains.'

They appeared to be as glad as I was of the altered circumstances. All the same, as I drew nearer to Rosemberg, passing through a region colonized by emigrants with no North American blood, hard-working farmers utterly devoted to the soil, with no thought for anything but the land, men, women and children fled at my approach, not waiting to be addressed. I felt I had once more wandered off the track of civilization.

I was surprised, in open country, by a bitterly cold storm of wind and rain that made me shiver till my teeth chattered and raised the bristles of the horses' hides. Their ears twitched miserably, as though they feared a return of the bad old days of mud, hail and all those other calamities we had suffered.

I was obliged to take refuge for the night in a churchyard, with earthen walls that protected us from the weather. The character of the place also rendered it safe from unwanted intruders. I found it an admirably secure and restful haven, though I had at first, when considering whether I should use it, felt rather frightened. I soon realised that there had been no foundation for my fears.

About halfway through that night the weather improved. I was able to doze off peacefully enough. From time to time I opened my eyes to glance by the light of the moon which appeared to be hanging immediately above my head at the horses as they grazed among the headstones. I had never seen

them so indifferent to their surroundings. The proximity
of those tranquil resting-places seemed, on the whole, to
have a reassuring effect.

At a later date newspaper articles of a sensational cast
recorded my nocturnal vigils in such places. Many people,
especially women, lifted their hands in horror. "Oh, the
poor thing!" they would cry. "Just think what she had to put
up with!"

For my part, I used to reflect that I would gladly have
substituted those nights among the tombs, which apparently
terrified so many people, for the hardships I had endured since
leaving Buenos Aires.

I made a detour to visit Houston and on quitting that city
found very few villages along my route. As a matter of fact,
for long stretches of the road there were none at all; as a
result I passed some rather restless nights.

I travelled along the great highway that runs, fairly near
the coast, from Brownsville to Orange in Louisiana, just
across the border of the State of Texas. The next big city after
Houston is Beaumont. At the latter place Young Luchador
lost a shoe and I entrusted his hoof to a gentleman who said he
understood shoeing. In spite of what he said, however, it
turned out that he was not much of an expert at the job.
He made a shocking mess of shoeing Young Luchador,
nailing the iron into his flesh and causing him to suffer agonies
for twelve days.

I left a trail of newspaper comment behind me in Texas.
It had begun in Brownsville with an article by Augusto
Aurirac in the local *Herald* for Sunday, the 20th December.
'Señorita Ana Beker, the Argentine Amazon, has at last
succeeded in crossing the frontier with her two horses and
will proceed either to-day, to-morrow or in a few days'
time on her way to Canada. She will undoubtedly be performing one of the most notable feats ever attempted, especially
at this time of the year. Though winter has not yet officially
set in here, it is already snowing hard in many districts of the
north. Blizzards, hurricanes and all the usual meteorological
symptoms of the season have been reported. One can imagine

what it will be like as soon as Christmas is over and the temperature falls still further. The day before yesterday, for example, five degrees below zero were recorded in Jefferson City.'

The writer's references to the cold were only too accurate. For some obscure climatic reason the cold we all suffered from at that time exceeded any I experienced throughout my whole ride: that fact alone will always make me remember northern Texas. For some days I rode with blue cheeks, my nose feeling like a solid block of ice and my lips chapped and cracked. Although the cold weather of the high table-lands of South America and elsewhere in that continent also overtook me in wild and lonely places, I never, or almost never, strange to say, felt so cold in those latitudes as in North America. Fury and Young Luchador had better chances than I had of warming up with exercise, as I often put them into a trot. Yet they too seemed quite benumbed with the cold.

Leaving my footsteps printed in the newspaper articles of Eleanor Galt, Bill Bazo, Nicholas Ochoa and other reporters, I passed from the State of Texas into that of Louisiana. At Lake Charles I was most hospitably received by the Cuban consul. But a little later, on the road to New Orleans, some twenty-five miles from the city, I experienced just the opposite treatment.

Quite respectable hotels and roadhouses are to be found along the great highways, especially in the neighbourhood of large cities. They are intended for the use of travellers. Rooms can be booked and garage space is available. I called at one of these places, just like any other traveller overtaken by night on his way, and asked for accommodation in the usual manner, requesting such services as any hotel is bound to provide. The first place I called at refused to take me in. So did the second. The proprietor of the third would not even let me approach the entrance. He seemed to be in a bad temper and contemplated me with an embittered and scornful expression.

"There's no room for you here. You're Spanish or Mexican or something like that, aren't you?"

"I'm Argentine. But wherever I come from you're bound to put me up. This is a hotel, isn't it?"

I spoke very slowly and could see that this unfriendly personage understood a few words and followed the drift of what I was saying to him. I stuck to my point, for I had no intention of being played up; it was out of the question for me to continue on my way that night, as there was heavy traffic on the road, dangerous in any case, and especially on account of the headlights of so many vehicles, which dazzled my horses.

Throughout my journey across the United States both I and my animals ran certain risks, which greatly increased as we approached New York, due to the excessive numbers of people and vehicles that crowded the highways. Our relatively leisurely rate of progress, in comparison with the speed of motor transport on the most frequented arterial roads, was in itself a danger. I had to keep an exceedingly sharp look-out in all directions to ensure that the automobiles did not run into or graze the horses as they passed. Many drivers showed a certain amount of annoyance at having to make violent efforts to evade the obstacle we presented. But most of the people in the vehicles merely shouted surprised or amused comments at me, good-humouredly enough. I was obliged to keep continually on the alert and moved in a state of perpetual anxiety.

I tried to explain to the infuriated hotel-keeper that it was impossible for me to continue on my way that night owing to the heavy traffic caused by the proximity of New Orleans. But so far from sympathising with my difficulties he grew even more obstreperous.

I told him that if he would not allow me to enter his hotel I should stay in the garden with my horses till daylight. To prove that I meant what I said I sat down on the grass, keeping hold of the reins of the animals. When the beasts began to trample down the plants he fell into a paroxysm of rage. He seized my arm and tried to pull me to my feet by main force. Not being able to manage it by himself he called to another man to drag the horses away. This second fellow, before I could stop him, snatched my whip and aimed a blow at me with it. I evaded this attack without retaliation, not considering that the moment had yet come to use my revolver. The proprietor, beside himself with fury, kept yelling: "Clear off into the woods! You go and sleep in the woods!" I asked who was the nearest legal authority and was told the sheriff.

They threatened to call the police. I retorted:

"All right, call them. The police are my friends!"

I went to see the sheriff, but he declared that as the hotel was run as a private enterprise he could not force the proprietor to admit any person to whom the said proprietor might object. I argued, for my part, that these hotels had been built at unfrequented spots along the road precisely for the benefit of such travellers as myself.

He shrugged his shoulders.

"Sorry, but——"

I uttered an exclamation of disgust and returned, with my horses, to the hotel where I had been refused admittance. I was ready to face anything that might happen.

The row had attracted the attention of the police by this time. Some of them came to meet me and said they would look after me. They simply took me to the local gaol, where they stabled the horses quite satisfactorily and then escorted me to the cells. When I saw the little grated windows I asked:

"Have I got to sleep among these criminals?"

"Yes," they answered. "Under the same roof, anyway."

They opened the door of one of the cells.

"Surely you have a proper bedroom somewhere!" I exclaimed.

In the end they showed me into a real bedroom, decently furnished. It was inside the prison building but did not come under prison rules!

CHAPTER XIX

ROAD TRAVEL IN THE UNITED STATES

IN New Orleans I was given one of the most enjoyable receptions in the history of my ride. I was accorded the freedom of the city in a ceremony I shall always remember; I was formally presented with a symbolical key, as is the custom in this independent and most congenial corner of North America. For the moment I became a popular figure on television and on the air. I participated, to my immense delight, in the festivities of the season, where my arrival was regarded almost in the light of a major event.

The Argentine consul, Señor Fernandez Mira, looked after me while I remained in New Orleans and requested when I left that I should be given an escort of two policemen up to the city boundaries to prevent my going astray in the enormous amount of traffic or getting myself run over.

I was very impressed by the various attractions of the city which is rightly called in the United States the Gateway to the South. I admired the characteristic architecture of the centre of the town, with its courtyards, gardens and beautifully designed window-gratings, no house ever having more than three floors. I also found impressive Jackson Square, formerly the ancient Spanish military parade-ground, and such survivals of the past as the Cathedral of St. Louis. I was delighted by the exuberant gaiety of the great Mardi Gras (Shrove Tuesday) carnival in which I was lucky enough to participate and I have vivid memories of the mighty Mississippi, or Father of Waters, the port of New Orleans being situated on its estuary, which flows into the Gulf of Mexico.

One of my most constant companions while I was in the city, a young teacher of Spanish, told me that the 2,500 miles of this famous river makes its course longer than that of the Nile and only inferior in extent to the bed of the Amazon. I was impressed by the huge concrete dykes built to prevent flooding and charmed by the gay spectacle of the excursion steamers and little paddle-boats towing their floating caravans of barges or lighters.

I rode for some time along the shores of the great river and when I grew tired slept for a while beside its delightful waters.

Greatly refreshed, like a vessel entering upon the most attractive stage of a voyage with swelling sails before a following wind, I crossed into the State of Alabama. Here it was the Chambers of Commerce of the larger towns that chiefly entertained me. At Birmingham the candidates for the mayoralty were conducting their respective campaigns and hurling defiance at each other. Nevertheless, they both overwhelmed me with attentions so that I too, though only a bird of passage, might form good opinions of them.

At Chattanoga, which is in Tennessee, a deputation of the local Argentine residents waited upon me; while I was still in New Orleans I had received a telegram from them advising me that they were making preparations for the stabling of my horses.

Among other invitations extended to me by my compatriots was a most enjoyable excursion on the funicular railway, which makes a vertical ascent for part of its course and enables one to obtain a bird's-eye view of magnificent scenery. At the summit of the mountain, which is also reached by a winding motor road, some of us arrived in a dazed condition after coming up by the almost vertical railway. We all inspected with pleasure the attractive town which had been built at this great altitude.

In the State of Tennessee, as in those of Mississippi and Alabama and many others, the schools were given a holiday in the towns I visited.

I shall tell my story from now on in much more summary fashion, for, though the distances I covered were great, a journey across the United States, where the land is more highly developed and more densely populated, does not provide the surprises, dangers and adventures to be met with in the forests, mountains and deserts of other latitudes. In other words, the traveller knows what he is in for and exactly where he has to go. Nothing in the States impressed me more than the excellent organisation of the country, the progressive spirit everywhere evident and the packed streets and soaring buildings of the great cities.

Nevertheless, miles are miles and I had to cover them step by step. Wind is wind and rain is rain; I was bound to encounter storms in such continuous travel by road and when I did there was nothing for it but to ride on, turning my head sideways so as not to be blinded by the rain and put up with the worst the weather could do till I was soaked through. Another great difficulty I had to contend with was my ignorance of the language. As I had to find the right roads and be careful not to miss them, this shortcoming of mine was a constant worry to me.

The occupants of the automobiles and buses that rushed past me on days when the weather was particularly atrocious stared at me as though I had gone mad. They would sometimes call out enquiries as they passed. I didn't understand the exact sense of the words. But it was obvious that they expressed amazement.

While I was riding through Virginia, on one of those days of appalling weather I have mentioned, a huge truck, painted red and towing a trailer of about the same size, slowed down as it caught me up. The men in it took immense pains to explain to me that no one ever travelled in such an extraordinary manner as I did and that they were sorry to see a woman facing such unpleasant conditions. I managed eventually to give them some idea of the reason for my behaviour and then they were more astonished than ever.

"Where are you going, then?" they asked me.

"To New York, for the time being," I answered.

"What, just like that? With those poor little brutes?"

They couldn't get over their amazement. In a country where mechanical horse-power is the means of transport, to use horses of flesh and blood for the purpose looks like a return to the days of the redskins.

They very good-naturedly offered to give the horses a lift in the trailer and myself in the cab as far as Culpeper, their destination. I did my best, though without success, to explain briefly why I could not accept this proposal. One of the men, who must have been a Texan or Californian, since he could speak a little Spanish, said to me:

"No one will see you doing it. No one will ever know."

"Maybe, but I shall know I've done it and I can't be guilty of such a fraud. It would be contrary to the whole spirit of my undertaking."

"O.K., then!" exclaimed the driver disgustedly. He accelerated, with a grimace that implied it was best to humour the crazy.

My entry into Washington, the historic centre of American independence, I regarded as a most solemn and memorable occasion. We formed, my horses and I, as we crossed the majestic bridge over the river Potomac, a group wholly exotic in appearance, though with something of the wayworn aspect of the early conquerors. The effect would really have been one of great solemnity if my worry over the enormous volume of traffic had not obliged me to keep continually on the alert and thus lose a certain amount of dignity.

In Washington I was besieged, with ever-increasing persistence, by Press, radio and television representatives. I also found there, after getting over my first fright at the traffic on the bridge, several people awaiting me whom I have to thank for according me a most cordial reception.

It was suggested that I might be able to call on President Eisenhower and efforts were made, in particular, to arrange a meeting with the Argentine ambassador, Señor Ezequiel Paz. The distinguished diplomat, however, was not in Washington at the time. I was received, nevertheless, with the most exquisite courtesy by his wife. I also attended a splendid reception at the Peruvian Embassy where I was overwhelmed with attentions I was far from deserving.

In my various expeditions I soon became familiar with this delightful city, which resembles a provincial city in its tranquil aspect. It is inhabited by 200,000 State officials, who lead a methodical and calm existence. The town is on the banks of the river Potomac but has spread far beyond its original boundaries which enclosed the Capitol. On the latter building a number of beautiful avenues converge, some being over thirty yards wide. The dome of the Capitol dominates a perspective of stone and marble edifices unbroken by sky-scrapers, which the municipality has prohibited from erection in the city. This feature of Washington distinguishes it from all the other large cities of North America. I was greatly taken with the abundance of green foliage and shade provided by so many trees.

The White House gave me a surprise. Though a fine stone building of good proportions, there is nothing palatially magnificent about it, but only the dignified simplicity of any private residence occupied by a well-to-do family. The attention which has been paid, to the preservation of the trees in the planning of the city, again gladdened my eyes when I beheld the remarkable marble edifice of the Capitol, sited among leafy gardens and fountains.

The students of Washington organised festivals in my honour and made much of me. Either by chance or perhaps by design I even found myself accompanied by so persistent an admirer that for some days I wondered whether two of us instead of one had been concerned in my ride. I judged my companion, from his youth and general behaviour, to be a student. He insisted on dressing as a Mexican Caballero and followed close behind me the whole time. His friends addressed him as 'Mexican' but he spoke perfectly correct English. To begin with, I met his gallantries with such composure as I could muster; afterwards I decided to fulfil my various engagements without troubling myself overmuch about his presence.

I lost him finally—and I take this opportunity to thank him for his care and attention to me—during my ride from Washington to New York, when I almost lost my wits as well. The tremendous volume of traffic was a great trial to my progress with the two poor animals. They were just as frightened, if not more so, as when they had to keep their balance in the forests on the trunks of fallen trees or had their flesh torn by the thorns of the undergrowth. The wind of the automobiles rushing past within a few centimetres of the horses' legs continually alarmed them. I tried to keep them as close together as possible, so as to present the smallest possible target to an onslaught which might well have had serious consequences. Young Luchador kept fairly quiet and allowed me to control him, while he gradually got used to the snorting of the interminable procession of automobiles. Fury, on the other hand, ran more and more risks in his panic of getting in their way. Once he gave a leap to avoid the onrush of a particularly fast vehicle and almost collided head on with a gigantic bus, of inordinate length, which only just missed his head and flank as he struggled to recover his balance. The side of the bus passed so close that the passengers nearest the windows started back with shouts of alarm, believing that Fury's muzzle was bound to touch them. There were many more similarly anxious moments; my arms ached with the strain of dragging at the reins to prevent the horses deviating a single inch from the narrow lane to which they had to keep.

On another occasion Fury actually bolted, while he was acting as pack-horse, hauling me after him as he tugged violently at the reins. The utter chaos that ensued, as automobiles braked, klaxons wailed louder and louder and police-whistles sounded, baffles all description.

I must freely confess that some drivers found themselves in difficulties on my account. But so far as the accident is concerned which occurred on Road 9 W—I mention it here by anticipation—that was not really my fault. The United Press Agency's report of this affair, published in a Red Hook newspaper, runs as follows: 'The Argentine Amazon, Ana Beker, was very nearly involved in a serious accident yesterday on Road 9 W, when two automobiles came into violent collision behind her. According to the police report a person travelling in one of the automobiles was immediately taken to hospital, suffering, it appears, from grave injuries. The Argentine Amazon, who is riding from Buenos Aires to

Ottawa, and was at the time traversing the final stage of her
15,000-mile journey on horseback, states:

' "I hope I shall not be blamed for this accident. I was riding
in the outer lane of the three making up the highway for
traffic in that direction." The lady from whose house Ana
Beker made this statement, some four and a half miles from
this town, has assured the United Press that the police merely
interrogated Ana in the course of their investigation of the
accident and did not claim that she was to blame for it. Ana,
after recovering from the shock, declared that she would
continue her ride and that the disaster in question was the
only one of the kind that had occurred during her journey.'

Once across the George Washington Bridge I entered the
huge metropolis which has so often been described in exhaus-
tive detail; the horses themselves appeared to be astonished
at the towering masses of cement and the incessant movement
of unending swarms of human beings. My companions and I
had never presented so violent a contrast with the general
aspect of our surroundings. Such a ride as ours through the
streets of New York could only be compared with some
advertisement for a circus or a film.

I owed much of the enjoyment to which I refer to newspaper-
men, the staff of the United Press and the radio organisations.
I was escorted almost the whole time by representatives of
the Paramount Company. They all stayed with me till I
was able to find suitable accommodation for my horses.

There were days on which I actually had to hide in order
to recuperate from the solicitous attentions of my friends
in the newspaper world. They turned up at the door of my
hotel at all hours of the night and in the early morning, eager
to ask me all sorts of questions and draw up a programme for
the day's activities.

I also owe a great deal of gratitude for the attention he
bestowed upon me to Julian Ortiz, the Argentine consul, son
of the famous actress Mecha Ortiz.

The vast metropolis itself will never be erased from the
multitude of impressions I received. I became conscious for
the first time of the miracle of the rock of Manhattan, with

its entrails pierced by tunnels and railways and the fabulous height of its buildings soaring into the sky. This once barren little island, hollowed out to its depths and mistress now of the air above it as well, shows what can be done by the immense industry of this human antheap.

I explored Broadway, which cuts across the city diagonally, and Fifth Avenue, which runs straight to the wonderful Central Park. I ascended to the top of the Empire State Building and traversed the streets leading from east to west and the avenues leading from north to south, including the splendid Riverside Drive overlooking the Hudson. My tiny figure, with its two accompanying little horses, counted for no more than a grain of sand in the vast maze of stone, steel cables and cement. In that colossal city the impressive artery of Broadway, cutting through Times Square, is by far the busiest area. The 'Great White Way', as it is called, resembles a cross-section of the whole world in miniature, where specimens of every sort of human being can be met with and all the various elements of a huge fair are simultaneously in feverish action. For a few moments I was thrilled by the uproar, the lights and the crowds, quite carried away and happy to form part of the scene. But soon I began to feel homesick for the quiet countryside of my native land, the tranquil plains of the pampas where I was born and grew up.

A few more days in the saddle—though they were long ones—and I had reached the boundary of this great North American country, the pride of modern progressive civilisation.

I was deeply and sincerely moved by all the kindness, generous attentions and moral and material support of myself and my horses which I received from the people of this great North American nation; I am sure I shall never forget them. Officials, members of private families, the police and many individuals whose names I never knew are all included in the general feelings of gratitude and respect I cherish for the United States.

CHAPTER XX

OTTAWA AT LAST

I REACHED the Canadian border at Champlain where I was invited to take part with my horses in a circus exhibition. This affair, which might have been simply an occasion of pride and glory for the animals, turned out to be a fresh source of suffering for them, especially for Fury. It happened that the proprietor of the circus stabled my horses in the same enclosure as that occupied by those of the many other equestrian performers. These animals objected to visitors at such close quarters; they were powerful brutes and launched an attack on my animals in order to drive them out. They inflicted a number of wounds on Fury with their hoofs and teeth.

Apart from my distress at the sight of Fury's injuries, they gave me trouble of a different kind, for I had hardly touched Canadian soil before I came under the displeasure of the veterinary inspector at the frontier, who invoked, with a frown, the regulations prohibiting the entry of defective animals into the country. It was not until after many notes had been taken and many arguments had been exchanged, accompanied by repeated close examination of the wounds, that the official vet., Dr. Jean Blais, consented to authorise Fury to cross the border. While the animals were standing tethered to a tree at the barrier itself, some motorists suddenly drove up with a terrific clatter. Fury shied, broke loose and galloped off at full speed in a direction the exact opposite to that leading into Canada. He was only caught after a considerable expenditure of time and trouble. When he had calmed down and been brought back to me someone remarked with a grin:

"He doesn't want to have anything to do with Canadians. He'd like to stay in the States."

At last we crossed into Canada, my final destination. Excitement made my heart beat harder than ever. I told Fury and Young Luchador that our sufferings would soon be over, that the rest of the ride would be a picnic, that it would only be like trotting or walking through a park.

It was true that for most of the time there was nothing to be seen along the road but evidence of the care and affection bestowed by man upon cultivation of the soil. The horses neighed with pleasure and replied to all my exclamations of satisfaction with an affirmative nod.

After less than three days spent in the saddle along those delightful roads I found myself in Montreal, one of the several large and beautiful cities of Canada. So as not to make too much of matters which have now become familiar to the reader I shall not dwell on the details of my cordial reception; I was amused to note, though, that in the attentions paid to me a good-humoured but incessant rivalry existed between members of the Press who spoke English and those who spoke French. For in Montreal every activity proceeds under the influence of one or the other of the characteristic culture expressed in these two languages, which persist side by side in the city.

One of the pleasures I experienced in Montreal was that of sending messages to various parts of the world over privately owned wireless transmitters. From Montevelo I was able to speak to the office of the President of the Argentine Republic and to persons who took a friendly and affectionate interest in me, such as members of the riding clubs in Columbia. I also sent messages to Cuba and other places in various latitudes, for the worldwide network covered by amateurs of radio transmission constitutes an effective means of disseminating good will over great distances.

I was nearing my final goal when I left Montreal for Ottawa. On reaching the beautiful capital of Canada I never stopped

till I came to the spot where I could write the longed-for word
'Finis' to the story of my adventure. My destination was the
door of the Argentine Embassy. I arrived there at four
o'clock in the afternoon of the 6th July, 1954. An enormous
crowd had collected in front of the Embassy. I was told that
it was the biggest ever seen there.

Inside the building microphones had been placed, belonging
to Radio Canada, so that I could broadcast to Latin America,
as well as to the English-and French-speaking populations of
Canada itself.

Everyone there seemed intensely anxious to entertain me,
take me home with them and invite me to a meal. To all their
entreaties I returned the question:

"What about my horses?"

Oats were immediately produced in great quantities to
regale the animals, who were the real heroes of the ride now
brought to a successful conclusion.

I was given quarters in one of the best hotels and provided
with a Cadillac to take me wherever I wanted to go. Young
Luchador and Fury were accommodated for the time being
in stables belonging to the Stevenson family, who made every
effort to compensate them, at this late hour, for their former
prolonged sufferings.

I listened to the broadcasts dealing with my ride, and heard
phrases such as 'the Argentine Amazon who has just crossed
the continent', 'We salute the heroine of this impressive
feat'. My conscience invariably reminded me that all these
compliments should really be shared with Young Luchador
and Fury and I passed on these eulogies to them. The
Equestrian Society presented me with a silver maple-leaf.
The Ottawa town councillors, Messrs. George Sican and
Wilbert Hamilton, asked and obtained my permission to pose
for their photographs holding the horses by the bridle. The
attitude of many municipal officials during my ride had
greatly encouraged me. The newspapers published a great
many photographs of myself in company with my two friends
the horses. The encouragement and congratulations offered
me by the Argentine ambassador, Señor Lucas Galigniana,

his charming wife, Dr. R. Cherry, President of the Equestrian Society and the Stevenson family whom I have already mentioned, confirmed my belief that the original inspiration for my ride had been a happy one.

I have only to add a few lines relating to my return. My two 'steeds' and she who had shared so many adventures with them embarked aboard the *Rio Tercero*, of the Argentine Merchant Marine. Now, I thought, we shall enjoy every comfort. A suitable little stable was erected on deck for the animals and I did not intend to let them out of my sight.

We left on the 27th August. At this very time, when I thought that all our troubles must now be over, the last of the shocks that I and my horses experienced together fell upon us. The return voyage had only just started when a storm of exceptional violence struck the *Rio Tercero*. The fury of the squalls sent everything on deck flying. The automobiles the ship was carrying turned over. The shelters erected for my animals swayed dangerously. The cables broke loose under the lash of the hurricane and the ship was driven out to sea. The horses, as usual when peril threatens, had felt a presentiment of the storm. Their instinct can generally be relied on in such cases. They assume a melancholy attitude, refuse to eat and do everything but speak and tell one that serious danger is imminent. On the other hand, as happened on that occasion, the delight evident in the gleaming of their eyes, the twitching of their ears and their whole behaviour had to be seen to be believed when they scented that land was near and caught sight of the first green patches and the first trees in the distance.

On the 27th September, 1954 we came to Argentina. At least, I thought, I was not returning without having accomplished what I had promised. Fate had been on my side, though perhaps I did not deserve it.

With a heart bursting with emotion and my eyes full of tears I once more set foot in my beloved country. I had achieved what I had set out to do and now I was back in Argentina, with the only witnesses of my past moments of joy or fear, the two noble beasts I was bringing home. They and I alone truly understand what we have faced together and remember how we felt at the times of our greatest enthusiasm, our deepest loneliness and our worst discouragements.

Other titles in the Equestrian Travel Classic series published by The Long Riders' Guild Press. We are constantly adding to our collection, so for an up-to-date list please visit our website: **www.thelongridersguild.com**

The Long Riders' Guild
The world's leading source of information regarding equestrian exploration!
www.thelongridersguild.com

CPSIA information can be obtained
at www.ICGtesting.com
Printed in the USA
BVHW032303050620
580728BV00001B/90